An African Pilgrimage on Evangelism

An African Pilgrimage on Evangelism

A Historical Study of the Various Approaches to Evangelism in Africa (100–2000 CE)

by

Dr. John Wesley Zwomunondiita Kurewa

Africa Ministry Series

DISCIPLESHIP RESOURCES
INTERNATIONAL

AN AFRICAN PILGRIMAGE ON EVANGELISM
A *Historical Study of the Various Approaches to Evangelism in Africa* (100–2000 CE)

Cover and interior design: Karin Wizer
Typesetting: Revelation Desktop Publishing
First printing: 2011

LIBRARY OF CONGRESS CATALOGING-IN-PUBLICATION DATA
ISBN 978-0-88177-603-4

Printed in South Africa by Salty Print, 14 Durham Avenue, Salt River

Contents

Preface

In 1970, David Barrett, who had served in East Africa since 1957 with the Church Missionary Society and was then secretary for research in the ecumenical research unit based in Nairobi, Kenya, predicted a total of around 351 million Christians (a 46 percent increase) by the year 2000 on the continent of Africa.[1] At the dawn of the twenty-first century a number of church leaders reiterated the impact of the phenomenal growth of Christians in Africa, Asia, and Latin America. In particular, Andrew Walls, former missionary in Sierra Leone, now Professor Emeritus at the University of Edinburgh, said, "Due to the growth of Christians in the developing world, the church's demographic center of gravity has shifted from the north and west to the south and east (Latin America, Africa, and Asia)."[2] Similarly, in his opening speech at the Eighth Assembly in Harare, Konrad Raiser, the General Secretary of the World Council of Churches at that time said, "By the early part of the 21st century, Africa promises to be the continent with the largest Christian population."[3] The Christian community envisioned in such predictions includes all versions of Christianity in Africa—Protestant, Roman Catholic, Orthodox, Coptic, African Initiative, and Pentecostal.

While there may be many reasons for the phenomenal growth of the church in Africa, two reasons stand out for our purpose here. First, emphatically, African religion from time immemorial taught belief in the One God, contrary to the views of the early missionaries to this continent who labeled the African people as heathens. There are many African Christians, including preachers, who still say that the African people did not know God until the advent of missionaries from western countries. But our forefathers knew something about God; they strongly believed that God created heaven and earth and all that we find on earth, and especially that God created humanity. Thus, Africa was like the good soil in Jesus' parable of the sower into which the gospel seed fell, easily geminated, grew up, and produced crops, multiplying thirty, sixty, or even a hundred times (Mark 4:8). Because of that continent-wide belief in God, Christianity found fertile ground in Africa.

Second, the churches in Africa regard evangelism as the heartbeat of ministry of the total mission of the church on this continent. If there is any one thing that brings the churches of Africa together, it is belief in the power and praxis of the ministry of evangelism—sharing Jesus Christ with others. That includes communicating the whole story of God's gracious dealings with humanity, offering transforming power for a new existence, and helping people realize they are a new people in Christ. This is what is bringing about this phenomenal growth of Christianity in Africa.

There is a third factor, however, that is important in initiatives to plant and grow Christianity in various regions of Africa throughout the centuries, and it is this: Christianity flourished wherever Christian communities, once founded, exercised courage to contextualize the new faith to their African culture and style of life. Such faith communities were able to establish strong foundations for themselves and embrace their new faith in Jesus Christ in their own ways. For that reason, they were able to resist the internal and external pressures that made other Christian communities collapse.

The purpose of this book is to explore such themes as these while providing a historical survey of the evangelistic approaches that were applied by the early Christian communities in the various countries and regions of Africa. With this exploration comes the hope of learning from their stories—their circumstances, successes, and failures. This critical examination of approaches to evangelism that have been employed by generations of earlier Christians, including Methodists, is more than an academic exercise; the ministries of past generations of Christians serve as a mirror for present faith communities. From their achievements and great contributions, we stand to gain fresh vision and courage for building and continuing our ministries of evangelism. From their mistakes or failures, we are warned and advised to look for relevant options.

Chapter 1

Evangelizing Egypt

Alexandria was the most important Egyptian city during New Testament times, and also the second most important city of the Roman Empire. Founded by Alexander the Great in 331 BCE, it was located near the delta of the Nile River and possessed the Museum with its Great Library and halls and gardens, the cultural capital of the Hellenistic world.[4] A quarter of its population was Jewish, and legend has it that Alexandria is where seventy-two Jewish scholars first translated the Hebrew Bible into Greek, creating the Septuagint.

Origin of Christianity

There is no clear information concerning the beginnings of Christianity in Egypt. Clement of Alexandria (born about 150 CE) is reported to have attested that Mark, the Evangelist, founded the church in Alexandria.[5] This view found support from Eusebius (260–339 CE), the early church historian from Caesarea. Eusebius cites Mark as the first man to set out for Egypt and preach the gospel he had written down, and first to establish churches in Alexandria.[6] The Coptic Church holds on dearly to this ancient tradition. They even go further in claiming that the Apostle Peter and Mark preached in Alexandria in 42 CE.[7]

Acts 18:24–28 reports the visit of Apollos, a learned man from Alexandria, to Ephesus where he came into contact with Priscilla and Aquila around 49–52 CE (judging by Paul's journeys). However, Hans Lietzmann points out that we do not know whether Apollos became a Christian in Alexandria or elsewhere. Otherwise, that would have been a significant clue in determining the presence of Christianity in Alexandria.

Lietzmann is of the view that Alexandria received Christianity in Rome.[8] That might have come about during the early part of the second century or during Hadrian's reign as Emperor (117–128 CE) when two distinguished Christian teachers arose in Alexandria, namely Basilides and Valentine. Later, Valentine moved to Rome and almost succeeded in becoming Pope. The two teachers belonged to the *Gnostic* movement,[9] a movement of people who believed they possessed secret knowledge (*gnosis*) for deliverance. Chadwick points out that during that early part of the second century, at the same time that the church of Rome struggled with Marcionites and the Valentines, it also sent a mission to help establish orthodox[10] Christianity in Alexandria.[11]

About the middle of the second century, Pantaenus emerged as a leader in Alexandrian Christianity. He was the first representative of orthodox Christianity known to be in Egypt.[12] He was also counted as an evangelist,[13] who wandered all over preaching the gospel. Eusebius described those evangelists as disciples whose hearts were smitten by the word of God, with an ardent passion for true and new philosophy or faith. Such evangelists left their homes behind in order to carry out the work of evangelists. They were ambitious to preach to those who had not yet heard the message of Jesus Christ, and to distribute to them the gospel copies that were already in circulation. Often, the evangelists ended up preaching in foreign countries where they would gather the converts and entrust the new disciples to the pastors; or they would appoint pastors if there were none to tend the new flocks.[14]

Evangelizing Alexandria

Pantaneus, an eminent teacher steeped in stoic philosophy, was also a fervent evangelist, as stated above. He "is said to have shown such a warm-hearted enthusiasm for the divine word that he was appointed to preach the gospel of Christ to the people of the East, and traveled as far as India,"[15] where he is reported to have found the Gospel of Matthew already in distribution.

Pantaenus established the *Catechetical School* in Alexandria during the second half of the second century. Second-century Egypt was a hotbed of Gnosticism, with eminent teachers of Gnosticism such as Basilides and Valentine in the city. Pantaenus's mission was to present an orthodoxy that was intellectually viable to the people of Alexandria.[16] Pantaenus, Clement of Alexandria, and Origen succeeded one another as head of the school, in that order.

The Catechetical School had a two-fold purpose. First, it instructed candidates for church membership. Teachers of the school knew effective evangelism went hand in hand with Christian education in order for the converts to grow toward Christian maturity in their faith. Second, the Catechetical School engaged in advanced theological and philosophical reflection with those who needed that approach. Frend makes the point that Pantaenus and Clement of Alexandria were two leaders who seriously took it upon themselves to evangelize the members of the Alexandrian aristocracy and to substitute an orthodox Christianity for the Gnosticism of the Egyptian teachers.[17] Origen, who succeeded Clement in about 202 CE, decided at an early age not to pursue studies of philosophy in order to concentrate on the Christian faith. To his surprise, some pagans approached him who wished to hear the word of God in relation to Hellenistic philosophies. One such person happened to be Heraclas, a philosopher, who later became Bishop of Alexandria.[18]

The Catechetical School instructed members of the church to understand orthodox Christian doctrines and the scriptures—the Old Testament and also the memoirs of the apostles, whose literature was circulating in cities such as Alexandria. The school also catered to those who wanted to engage in theological reflection on the Christian faith in the context of the Hellenistic philosophies of the day. This is what we would consider theological or seminary education. It is no wonder the school produced great leaders such as Pantaenus, Clement, and Origen.

Clement of Alexandria was born of non-Christian parents, probably in Athens around 150 CE. Having been converted as an adult, Clement went on a long spiritual pilgrimage. After seeing many teachers, Clement settled in Egypt as a pupil of Pantaneus,[19] whom he described as "a truly Sicilian bee."[20] Clement became Pantaneus's successor around 190 CE. Clements' main contribution was in teaching the Christian believers not to reject their culture's philosophical ways and thought forms in order to be Christian. Rather, he assisted his pupils to use their cultural and philosophical wealth in order to interpret the Christian faith for themselves. Clement is known for embracing Greek philosophy as of divine origin.[21] Like Paul, who had spoken of the Law of Moses as a *paidagogos* (custodian, schoolmaster, disciplinarian, or tutor) until the coming of Christ, Clement attributed a similar role to Greek philosophy.

> Even if Greek philosophy does not comprehend the truth in its entirety and, in addition, lacks the strength to fulfill the Lord's command, yet at least it prepares the way for the teaching which is royal in the highest sense of the word, by making him ready to receive the truth (Storm., I 80).... Greek philosophy, as it were, provides for the soul the preliminary cleansing and training required for the reception of the faith, on which foundation the truth builds up the edifice of knowledge. (Storm., VII, 20)[22]

Clement of Alexandria was a good example of a great Christian thinker who attempted to use his knowledge of philosophy to interpret the Christian faith, especially to those who were of the Hellenistic and philosophical background, which was common in Alexandria in those days. He showed that new converts do not have to be alienated from their cultural background in order to be Christians. However, in 202–203 CE, a persecution broke out under Septimius Severus in Alexandria that led to the arrest of the Jews and Christians. After Clement fled from Alexandria, Origen, who was still under eighteen years of age, was selected to be Clement's successor as head of the catechetical school.

Origen's father, Leonides, who had been a Christian for only a few years before his death, took delight in instructing his son in the scriptures. But Leonides was arrested and suffered martyrdom during Severus's persecution. Origen had also sought to offer himself for martyrdom and would have, had his mother not succeeded in hiding his clothes. He had, it is reported, "a zeal intense beyond his years."[23] Origen contributed enormously as a teacher in relating Christian faith and the study of Greek philosophy, and especially as an interpreter of the Bible (Old Testament), although his method of interpretation was allegory. Origen was a lay teacher, yet many bishops in the church had great respect for his scholarship, and so invited him to lead Bible study and to interpret the Christian faith in their churches. As head of the Catechetical School, he assigned the teaching of the less mature pupils to an assistant named Heraclas,[24] who was mentioned earlier on. Origen is regarded as the last great teacher (in the order of the charismatic teachers who were received by the church universally) in the history and life of the early church. Probably Origen had the greatest impact on the universal church as a biblical teacher and theologian of his time.

Origen greatly impacted his students, so much so that several of them suffered martyrdom. A female student martyr, Potamiaena, having already been tortured, suffered dreadful agonies at the hands of a judge named Aquila, who finally threatened to hand her over to the gladiators.[25] Yet, Potamiaena would not give up her faith in Christ. After the judge pronounced her death sentence, one soldier, Basilides, showed her sympathy by driving away the people surrounding her. He then seized her arm and led her away to execution. Potamiaena accepted Basilides's sympathy for her and gave him encouragement. She told Basilides that when she was gone away, "she would ask her Lord for him, and it would not be long before she repaid him for all that he had done for her."[26] She then was executed.

A few days later, Basilides's fellow soldiers asked him to take an oath, which he refused to do on the grounds that he was Christian. When asked by those close to him the reason for such amazing behaviour, he explained that three days after her martyrdom, Potamiaena had stood before him in the night and put a wreath about his head. She said that she had prayed for him to the Lord, and had obtained her request, and that before long the Lord would place him before her side. Upon hearing that message, Basilides was baptized. He was beheaded the following day. It is reported that "many other citizens of Alexandria accepted the teaching of Christ in a body, as Potamiaena appeared to them in dreams and called them."[27]

Christianity Along the Nile Valley

Alexandrian Christianity spread along the Nile Valley to the kingdoms of Nubia and Makuria, part of what is now Sudan, and the kingdom of Alwa, part of what is now Ethiopia. It may be helpful to understand a bit about the farming settlements on the banks of the Nile River. The desiccation[28] of the Sahara region from about 3000 BCE caused the Sahara population to move and settle on the banks of the Nile River. Its delta and valley upriver consisted of some of the richest soil for agricultural purposes on the continent. Even long before the desiccation of the Sahara region, the Egyptians were considered farmers—the earliest farmers. Archaeologists discovered small composites on the edges of the floodplain, which is indication that at some previous period in history people fished the Nile for catfish. Those Egyptians also planted wheat, barley, and other cereals in dump ponds of the Nile, as well as keeping sheep and goats. Therefore, the concentration of the population of Egypt would be found along the Nile Valley with cities, small towns, and several villages.

Beginning in the middle of the third century, there was a mass turning away from the old religions to Christianity in Egypt.[29] That movement must have begun with Christianity spreading from Alexandria and, as already mentioned, extending along the Nile Valley. In Alexandria, the population primarily spoke Greek, and Christianity used the Greek language as its medium of communication. We have noted that leaders such as Clement of Alexandria and Origen used Greek philosophy as part of their curriculum in the Catechetical School in order to reach persons of that language and cultural orientation with the gospel. But as Christianity spread along the Nile River Valley, it touched the Copts. The word *Coptic* refers to an ancient Egyptian language, and the native Egyptians were known as *Copts*. Christianity found its way from the Greek-speaking population in Alexandria to the Coptic-speaking population up the Nile River Valley.

The church provided the masses of the population with literature in the speech of everyday life,[30] which was the Coptic language. Coptic language was spoken in four dialects from the third to the tenth century. The New Testament was translated into each of the four dialects, and the language is still used in the liturgy of the Coptic Church today.[31] The translation of the scriptures into non-Greek vernaculars or Coptic language was indeed an act of laying the foundation of a native Egyptian (Coptic) church[32]; it was one way of indigenizing the church of Egypt in the Nile Valley. No wonder the masses received Christianity with great enthusiasm.

However, there could have been a number of other reasons for the masses turning to Christianity. One possibility, already noted, is that there was a persecution that could have drawn people to Christ instead of Osiris.[33] The courage of Christians to become martyrs was a great witness to Christ by his followers. Another reason was the official religion's role in the suffering of the peasant people. For example, temples were associated with forced taxation. Additionally, the women played a key role in evangelizing households to the Christian faith.[34]

About the middle of the third century, Christianity in Egypt took a new turn. Ascetic life or asceticism[35] thrived in the eastern desert of Egypt. The persecution of people by emperors such as Decius (249–251 CE) and Diocletian (284–311 CE), was severe. Many martyrs faced atrocious suffering to an extent that "the executioners were exhausted and the axes worn out."[36] The martyrs who fled into the desert became known as "the desert people." There were several reasons for going into the desert. Some people were running away from the intolerable burden of imperial taxation; others feared persecution. Still others sought God and the ideal of Christian perfection there.[37] That promoted the spirit of asceticism, which led to the founding of the monasteries in the Egyptian desert. The desert became dotted with monks and hermits.

Paul of Thebes was the first hermit in the desert around 250 CE.[38] It is said that having left his home city for the desert at a time of persecution, Paul discovered the treasures within the desert silence and never returned.[39] Similarly, one Sunday morning in 271 CE, a man named Antony heard a voice say, "If you want to be perfect, go, sell your possessions and give to the poor... Then come, follow me" (Matt. 19:21). After putting aside provisions for his sister, Antony headed off to the desert, where he stayed and supported himself by manual work. He began what is considered the first monastery in the history of the Christian Church. About 310 CE, another Egyptian young man named Pachomius was converted and baptized. He had already begun practicing asceticism before he was baptized. At Tabennisis, about 320 CE, Pachomius heard a voice, "Stay here, and make a monastery, for many will come to thee and become monks."[40] Indeed, more and more people came out from the cities into the desert. They emphasized the concept of self-sufficiency, which led them to be involved in manual work. They grew their own food in gardens, made mats and baskets, fed the wandering poor in the desert, sent food to prisons, and fed the poor of Alexandria.[41]

The institution of monasteries spread throughout the church in eastern countries such as Palestine and Syria, and in western countries such as Italy and others. Europe and the rest of the world owes a debt of gratitude to Antony and Pachomius for universities, schools, and hospitals. These came about through the system of monasteries that came out of Egyptian Christianity, which was very innovative.[42] The adoption of the monasteries was one way the Egyptian church indigenized Christianity.

The Coptic Church

We have already noted that Christianity spread further south, up the Nile Valley from Alexandria. It happened that in the fourth century the church, both in the West and East, was involved in a theological controversy regarding the nature of Christ, whom Christians in their worship addressed as God. The Christological development that acknowledged Christ as God needed immediate clarification concerning the relationship of God the Father and God the Son. This controversy seriously divided the Church, especially in the East. Some theologians took the position that Christ as the Son could not be equal to God or co-eternal with the Father, and therefore could not be addressed as God. Those who opposed this view argued that if Jesus Christ was not co-equal and co-eternal, and not God, then our salvation is not from God but from a human being, meaning the claim of salvation through Jesus Christ was false. Two clergymen of Alexandria led the controversy, Arius, an elder, took the former position, and Athanasius, a deacon, took the latter position.

The controversy led Emperor Constantine to call for the Nicea Council of the Church in 325 CE. The decision at Nicea, later finalized at the Council of Chalcedon (451 CE), was that Christ is "*true God, and at the same time, true man.*"[43] Essentially, they resolved that in Christ were two complete natures—one divine and the other human. The Egyptian church and almost all the rest of the Eastern church were not happy with the Chalcedon decision. They felt the divine nature of Christ had been compromised; they did not accept this Christology. Those who opposed the Chalcedon decision taught *Monophysitism*, a Christology that held *there was only one dominant nature in Jesus after the Incarnation and it was divine.*[44]

Gradually, there emerged a self-conscious Coptic nationalism, opposed to both Constantinople and to the Melkite Orthodox Greeks of Alexandria. The schism or split came about when the church in Egypt around the middle of the fifth century had two patriarchs, one Coptic patriarch representing Monophysite Christianity and a Melkite patriarch representing Orthodox Christianity.[45]

Arab Conquest of Egypt

In the meantime, the Arabs had already conquered Syria, Iraq, and Persia in January 640; Egypt, which was still under control of the Byzantine forces, became the next target. By 641, the Arabs were in control of Egypt. Alexandria revolted in 645, but was retaken in 646. However, Nubia in the south signed a treaty of peace on condition of payment, enabling it to survive as a Christian kingdom (Coptic Church) until the thirteenth century.[46]

Summary

There are lessons that the church in Africa today may learn from the Egyptian Christianity of the first through the seventh century.

First, Alexandrian Christianity was patterned on the Matthean Great Commission method of evangelism (see Matt. 28:19–20). The church of Alexandria made Christian disciples by using a double track: (a) they evangelized the people and baptized the converts; (b) they taught the converts so that they would understand the Christian faith through the Catechetical School (theological education).

Second, the church of Alexandrian Christianity, which found itself in a Greek-speaking population, adopted programmes that met the needs of that population. They established the Catechetical School, to provide *theological education* for the two groups in the church: (a) those seeking an orthodox understanding of Christian doctrines and scriptures (Old Testament plus the memoirs of the apostles whose writings were circulating in big cities such as Alexandria), and (b) those seeking theological reflection on Christian faith in the context of the Hellenistic philosophies of the day. The latter was what we today would consider theological or seminary education.

Third, the church in Africa today can learn from the fact that the

Catechetical School of Alexandria provided theological education to the whole church, not a select few. The African church inherited from our missionary-mentors, an understanding of *theological education* that relates primarily to those who are pursuing studies for ordination. T*heological education,* however, is the knowledge that the whole church—the body of Christ—understands as its faith and that the church needs to impart to both the leadership and the membership. The whole church is in need of theological education.

Fourth, Alexandrian Christianity acknowledged Hellenistic thinking and Greek philosophy as the part of the culture through which to communicate Christ and Christian faith. The Catechetical School, for example, did not condemn its cultural inheritance and philosophical thought forms, nor did it require converts to reject their culture in order to become Christian. Instead, it used the prevailing philosophical medium to convey the gospel and explain how Christ fulfilled in real life the truth that their philosophies already knew in general. Clement of Alexandria, for example, embraced Greek philosophy, though he was also able to point out its limitations. He attributed to it the same role that Paul attributed to the law of Moses, the role of a *paidagogos* (custodian, schoolmaster, disciplinarian, or tutor) until the coming of Christ (see Gal. 3:24–25).

In contrast, Christianity in Africa from the nineteenth century to this day has rejected African culture as unchristian. African church leaders, especially from missionary-established churches, denounce some of the pillars of African cultural structures, such as the *n'anga* institution, which is renowned for its medicinal and healing service in African society. The irony in this is that today some African nations are securing traditional medicine from China and India to treat people who suffer from malaria and other ailments. Does that not teach us a lesson? If Christianity were to accept the *n'anga* institution, it could surely be redeemed with the help of our many African doctors who are scientifically trained, together with the efforts of African governments to integrate health services in our nations. As in the old days, people could—even through the church—be taught the characteristics of good herbalists and traditional healers.

Fifth, the Egyptian church was able to contextualize the Christian faith to its geo-social situation. In the south and the Nile Valley, the church adapted itself to the culture of the people, by using the Coptic language and providing literature in the vernacular language of the people. Elsewhere, Egyptian Christianity adapted itself to the desert conditions of the people, such as "the people of the desert" who fled either from heavy taxation of the cities or persecution. This was the origin of the monastic Christian life in the Egyptian Desert, a phenomenon that spread to the churches of the East and the West.

Sixth, Alexandrian Christianity suffered many martyrs. Origen is known for preparing young people to face martyrdom without fear, as an opportunity for witnessing for Christ. Of course, martyrdom should not be sought or undertaken for its own sake. Today, martyrs seem to be associated only with Christians of the past. Yet the history of many of our African nations, even in the post-independent era, is no stranger to martyrdom. As the African church recognizes many of the martyrs in the universal history of the church and the missionary-martyrs, we also need to remember recent martyrs, some of whom we know well, who died for their faith and for the love of their people. The churches ought to celebrate their lives, write their biographies, and through Christian education teach young disciples about the witness of such martyrs. Above all, Christianity, taking its cue from Origen of Alexandria, must continue teaching and preparing its adherents for fearless and victorious Christ-like living more than martyrdom.

Chapter 2

Evangelizing North Africa

Christian North Africa from the first through the seventh centuries covered the coastal northern region of North African countries known to us today as Libya, Tunisia, Algeria, and Morocco. There is a sense in which North Africa became a hub of Christianity until the seventh century CE.

The historical background of these countries is that as early as 1110 BCE, the Phoenicians from Levant (region east of the Mediterranean, including all countries bordering the sea between Greece and Egypt) founded trading stations in Morocco. The Phoenicians were interested in the gold, silver, and tin of the Atlas Mountain mines. The influx of the Phoenicians to North Africa led to the founding of Carthage (modern Tunis) in 814 BCE, and with time Carthage became a trading settlement. After Rome became the power of the day in the third century BCE, her conflict with Carthage led to three wars, the first in 264–261 and the second in 209–206, the results swaying in favour of Rome. The third war was known as the Punic War in 201–146 BCE, which Rome launched against the Berbers, leading to the destruction of Carthage. Although local resistance continued for some time, by 25 CE Augustus had occupied North Africa.[47] Following the conquest of Carthage by the Romans in 146 BCE, the coastal region of North Africa became known as Roman North Africa. The Romans rebuilt a new Carthage on the same site of the old city, and new provinces were established, namely, Mauritania, Numidia (northern Algeria), Cyrenaica, and Africa in Tunisia, "which took its name from the local *Afri* and gave its name to a continent."[48]

In this region Rome seized land from the Berbers[49] and parceled it to the Roman soldiers and other Italians who were interested in becoming landowners in North Africa as colonists. Rome drew the wild animals needed for the circus games as well as agricultural supplies from North Africa. This led to the creation of splendid cities, whose ruins show a number of theaters, baths, temples, markets, and paved streets—evidence of the wealth that those landowners enjoyed in the region. The citizens of the region, both the colonists and Berbers, were granted Roman citizenship. Indeed, many indigenous North Africans, such as the Berbers, who wanted social mobility in the Roman world, took that path.[50]

The development of North African Christianity must be understood against the background of the Roman rule in the region. During the Roman occupation of North Africa, the countries mentioned above were known as Cyrenaica, Africa, Numidia, and Mauritania. By the first century Christianity had reached Libya (Cyrenaica), by the second century Tunisia (Africa), and by the fourth century Algeria (Numidia) and Mauretania (Morocco).

North African Leaders in New Testament Times

One noticeable factor in our study of the history of the early church is that Africans from North Africa were among those in the forefront of the Christian movement from its origin. The following serve as examples.

First, a man from Cyrene, an important city of Libya, by the name Simon, the father of Alexander and Rufus, is reported to have been forced to carry the cross of Jesus of Nazareth to the place of his crucifixion (Mark 15:21). There was a large population of Jews in Libya, and it is possible that Simon was not only a Berber but also a Jew. Simon, with other Jews from Libya, may have been in Jerusalem then for the celebration of the Passover Festival. (Could Simon have been one of the Jews of Cyrene referred to in Acts 6:9?) A person condemned to death was often forced to carry his own cross to the place of crucifixion. Jesus, who had been weakened by flogging and lack of sleep the previous night, could not carry his cross. Simon came to Jesus' rescue.

One wonders why Simon is reported to have been forced to carry the cross of his Jesus! Going back into the Old Testament history, about six hundred years previously, we find a similar situation when the prophet of God Jeremiah is rendered hopeless. He was thrown into a cistern, a dry well, for telling King Zedekiah the truth he did not want to hear (Jer. 37:16ff). Yet, it was a Cushite (an African), Ebed-Melech, an official in the royal palace, who came to rescue Jeremiah from the cistern where he had been left to die (Jer. 38:7ff). Ebed-Melech did what he had to do out of his big heart! Relating that incident of Jeremiah and Ebed-Melech, a Cushite, to that of Jesus of Nazareth and Simon, a Berber, raises a question: Was Simon, an African who probably knew what Ebed-Melech had done for the prophet Jeremiah, forced to carry the cross of Jesus of Nazareth? Or, could he have been influenced by Jesus who told stories about the Good Samaritan (Luke 10:30ff)? It would have been helpful to have heard what Simon may have said about his role in carrying that cross.

Second, God-fearing Libyans were present on the day of Pentecost in Jerusalem, 28 May, 30 CE, witnessing the downpour of the Holy Spirit, and the birth of the Church of Jesus Christ (see Acts 2:10).

Third, when persecution broke out against the church of Jerusalem after the stoning of Stephen, leading all except the apostles to scatter, Luke makes reference to men from Cyprus and Cyrene (Libya). These men went to Antioch and were the first ones to preach the good news about the Lord Jesus to the Greeks (Acts 11:20).

Fourth, Luke makes another reference regarding men from Libya, who were prophets and teachers in a church at Antioch. They were Simeon called Niger, and Lucius of Cyrene, along with Barnabas, Paul, and Manaen. Some scholars speculate that the same Simon mentioned by Mark and Luke (Luke 23:26) could have been the Simeon called Niger that we now find in Antioch.[51] The name Niger also suggests that he was not only Libyan, but also a Berber.[52] What a witness that would have been—Simon, a Berber or an African, carrying the cross of his Master, Jesus, to the place of his crucifixion on Mount Calvary. In writing to the saints in Rome, Paul must have found it compelling to send his greetings to Rufus, Simon's son (Rom. 16:13).

Fifth, Victor I, the first African Pope (189–199), who succeeded St. Eleutherius as bishop of Rome, was a North African. Victor is known for the Easter Controversy. The Eastern churches celebrated Easter at different times. By threatening excommunication to those who would not comply with celebrating at the time agreed to by the rest of the churches, he was able to harmonize the celebration and to magnify the authority of the Holy See.[53] That could be the reason some scholars consider him the first Pope.[54]

Origin of Christianity

Though we have much evidence that the Libyan Christians in Palestine, Antioch, and Rome were missionary minded, we still do not know who brought Christianity to North Africa. One could speculate that Christianity traveled to North Africa both southwards from Rome and westwards from Egypt.[55] The known Christian history of the Libyan church begins dramatically in 180 CE with the martyrdom of twelve Christians (five woman and seven men) from the small village of Scilli, near Carthage:

> One carried his bag, "books and letters of Paul, a just man." The kindly Roman proconsul who presided at their trial did not desire their death. He pointed out that he, too, was a religious man, and suggested that they take 30 days to think things over, but the Scilli martyrs needed no time for reference: "Today, we are martyrs in heaven. Thanks be to God." The words resound through a North African Christian history dominated by a passion for martyrdom.
>
> *The Passion of Saints and Felicity* is one of the moving documents left from the first centuries of the Church. Perpetua is one of the four early women Christians in the ancient world whose writings have survived. Most of the

> text in her prison journal was "...written in her own hand and according to her own perceptions. She was a member of a prosperous family, aged twenty-two, married with a baby boy. Her father was a pagan; the journal describes his despairing attempts to save his beloved child from the death she embraced. She was martyred with others [after refusing to sacrifice to the Roman gods], among them Saturus, and her friend, the slave, Felicity, also the mother of a new baby."[56]

On the manner of persecution:

> Vibia Perpetua and her servant friend, Felicitas ... were led into the arena where some Christian men were torn to pieces by animals as a public spectacle. The women were stripped naked, but when the crowd was offended by the authorities exposing the ladies' nakedness, Vabia and Felicitas were given over to a bull which was let loose into the area. The bull tossed and wounded the women but did not kill them, so gladiators were ordered to kill them with swords. This persecution took place on February 2, 203.[57]

Vibia Perpetua is said to have left a legacy of principles in the tradition of the North African church. All the responses she displayed to her persecutors were credited to the guidance of the Holy Spirit. For example, she witnessed to the fact that her baptism was a baptism into the death of Christ, and that she requested nothing from the baptismal waters except the suffering of the flesh. She claimed to have visions of Paradise, and to have conversed with the Lord, all of which gave her the courage to face the suffering of death in the amphitheatre.[58]

Great Leaders of Christianity

Tertullian shares with us some insights concerning the strength and suffering caused by the persecution of the church in North Africa during the early part of the third century. Tertullian was born to a pagan Roman family in Carthage around the year 160 and died after 220 CE. He was educated in rhetoric and law in Rome, and became a Christian possibly around 207. He became disillusioned with the church authorities and at one point spoke in favour of Montanism.[59] He was a Carthaginian presbyter—one of the born rebels of history. He is said to have revolted successively against the army mess life of his father's household, and he revolted against the purposelessness of Roman provincial culture. As a Christian, he revolted against the laxness and complacency of the church in Rome and Carthage, and finally against Montanism, a sect he had joined for some time.[60]

Tertullian was the first important Christian to write in Latin. He is considered the father of Latin Christianity and the founder of Western theology. He coined the Latin term trinitas, meaning trinity—God the Father, God the Son, God the Holy Spirit. He wrote more than thirty works, which fell under three main groups: apologetic works; dogmatic/ anti-heretical works; and practical works. In the most famous of his apologetic works, which is simply called *Apology*, Tertullian argued skillfully against the injustice of condemning believers solely because they were Christians. As Tertullian wrote in his *Apology* 37:

> We are but of yesterday and we have filled all your places—cities, islands, forts, market places, the very camp, tribes, companies, palaces, senate, [and] forum. We have left nowhere to you except the temples of your gods.[61]

Christianity in North Africa continued to grow. By the end of the second century, Carthage had a powerful bishop, Agrippinus, who summoned the Council of North African Bishops in 220 CE to debate the rebaptism of those baptized by heretics. The Council agreed to the rebaptism as a measure of reconciliation in the life the church.[62] During the third century, the church in Libya had reached the Atlantic coast with hundreds of churches in between. All that expansion of Christianity in North Africa took place in spite of the persecution of the Christians. In *Apology* 50, Tertullian wrote:

> Your cruelty (against us) does not profit you, however exquisite. Instead, it tempts people to our sect. As often as you mow us down, the more we grow in number. The blood of the Christians is the seed (of the church)… The very obstinacy which you criticize teaches for us.[63]

Tertullian shared a splendid sarcasm in which he pictured the Lord on the Day of Judgment saying that "while he had entrusted the Gospel once and for all to the Apostles, he had thought better of it now and made some changes to suit the heretics…."[64]

Caecilian Cyprian was another prominent leader of the North Africa Church. He was born into an upper-class pagan family. He taught rhetoric at Carthage, and became a Christian about 245–246 CE. The following is a statement of his conversion:

> I was myself entangled and constrained by the very many errors of my former life that I could not believe it possible for me to escape from them…. But when the stain of my earlier life had been washed away by the help of the water of birth (baptism)…and the second birth had restored me so as to keep me a new man…what before had seemed difficult was now easy.[65]

Cyprian wrote two important books. In *The Lapsed*, Cyprian makes the point that the lapsed Christians during the period of persecution were to be readmitted after a period of penance. In his second book, *On the Unity of the Church*, Cyprian points out that the church cannot, of its very nature, be divided—that the unity of the Church is a given fact. He said it was not possible to divide the church, only to leave it. However, Cyprian's understanding of the unity of the Church was focused on bishops: "You ought to know that the bishop is in the church and the church in the bishop. If anyone is not with the bishop, he is not with the church."[66]

Persecution of the Christians in North Africa intensified especially during the middle of the third century by two Emperors—their persecution known as the Decian (249–251) and Valelian (253–259). The basis for the persecution was the imperial edict requiring all citizens to sacrifice to the Roman gods. For Christians to comply with the edict would have resulted into idolatry. Thus, they chose martyrdom. Cyprian, who had served as Bishop of Carthage for about ten years, suffered martyrdom during the Valelian persecution in 258.[67] Again, after there had been peace for a while, the Diocleatian persecution broke out, lasting between 303 and 313. Christians were ordered to hand over their copies of the scriptures and their church buildings were burned.

Aurelius Augustine, the Bishop of Hippo, is considered the greatest Christian theologian since the Apostle Paul. He was born at Thagaste, in modern Algeria, of a pagan father and a Christian mother, Monica, in 354. As a student at Carthage, Augustine studied philosophy, but later turned to Manicheism, a Persian religion with two ultimate principles or gods—Light and Darkness. As a candidate for baptism, he had studied the Old Testament, which he reacted to as unspiritual. In 384, he was appointed professor of rhetoric at Milan, where he began reading some neo-Platonists. In Milan, Augustine began to attend to Ambrose's sermons, which reconciled the Old Testament with Platonist spirituality. He became intellectually convinced of the truth of Christianity, but found the idea of celibacy a hindrance.

As he became torn between the two ways, one day he rushed into the garden where he heard the voice of a child crying, "Take up and read." Augustine opened Paul's letter to the Romans at 13:13–14:

> Let us behave decently, as in the daytime, not in orgies and drunkenness, not in sexual immorality and debauchery, not in dissension and jealousy. Rather, clothe yourselves with

> the Lord Jesus Christ, and do not think about how to gratify the desires of the sinful nature.

Augustine shares that as he finished reading the quotation, "the light of confidence flooded into my heart and all the darkness of doubt vanished."[68] He was baptized by Ambrose the following Easter. He returned to Africa in 388 and went into a monastery. In 391, as he was visiting Hippo, he was spotted and forcibly ordained priest. When the bishop of Hippo died in 396, Augustine succeeded him until his death in 430.

Augustine is known for many achievements. For instance, he composed pop songs, fought against Donatism, and developed the doctrine of the invisible church. He promoted the validity of sacraments even administered by Donatists. In his fight against Pelagianism, Augustine understood faith as a gift of God, the work of grace. He advocated that "reason seeks to understand what faith believes," and expounded the doctrine of the Trinity more clearly than anyone before him. After Rome fell to the barbarians in 410 CE, between 413 and 427 Augustine wrote *The City of God*, a book in which he argues against the accusation that the unprecedented disaster of the fall of Rome was to be blamed on Christianity—that the pagan gods were angry because they were not being worshipped. Augustine responded by saying the pagan gods did not provide anything; moreover, Christianity does not offer temporal, worldly success but inner peace and an eternal destiny.

The second Church Council to resolve the New Testament canon met in Carthage, 397 CE, under the leadership of Augustine, Bishop of Hippo, and approved as canonical the twenty-seven books of the New Testament as we know them today. That shows how important Carthage had become, and above all the role the church in North Africa played in the early history of the Church.

Arab Conquest of North Africa

The Arab conquest of North Africa took place in the seventh and eighth centuries, partly as a result of Rome falling into the hands of the Barbarians in 410, and partly as an internal conflict within the Roman North Africa region itself. The fall of Rome meant Roman rule over the known world had come to an end. Rome had lost grip of its worldwide empire. The Arabs who had been waiting in the desert made an alliance with the Berbers of raiding and violence. Not only did the Arabs take over North Africa politically, their conquest also ended the seven- or eight-century era of Christianity in the region. Furthermore, the Arabs crossed the Mediterranean Sea to raid Spain as well. Gradually, Islam became the religion of North Africa.

Summary

We can make several observations concerning the church in North Africa. First, North African Christianity is marked by its strong participation in the origin of Christianity. The list includes: Simon, who carried the cross of Jesus; the Libyans, who were present in Jerusalem on the day of Pentecost; the Libyans and Cypriots, who pioneered preaching the gospel to the Greeks; the Libyans, who rubbed shoulders with Barnabas and Paul as prophets and teachers at Antioch; and Victor, Bishop of Rome (189–199). African church leaders today, no less than in the past, need to participate in ecumenical church gatherings, contribute towards the church's discernment of God's mission, and share in its world mission, ministry, and evangelism.

Second, the church of North Africa spread to several Berber villages, and "every town, almost every village had its bishop."[69] We witness a similar phenomenon in Africa today as Christianity is spreading to both the rural and urban areas. Bishops of mainline churches are multiplying with each decade, and so are the number of bishops of African Initiative churches and Pentecostal churches. This doubling of the number of bishops could be a good sign of the growth of the church, but it could also be a bad sign of numerous splits due to power struggles.

Third, the church of North Africa was the church of martyrs. We are reminded of the dedication of Perpetua, Saturus and her friend Felicity the slave, Cyprian the Bishop of Carthage, and many others. North African Christianity was probably marred by martyrdom, an issue we have already discussed under Christianity in Alexandria.

Fourth, the church in North Africa produced some of the great leaders of the church universal, such as Tertullian, Cyprian, Augustine, and many others. One of the most interesting features about these leaders is their personal testimony about how they began their Christian lives. Further, it is important to note Tertullian's disillusionment, first with orthodox Christianity and later on with Montanism. There seem to be a number of people today who are disillusioned with orthodox Christianity in our churches. For that reason, some people change their loyalty from one denomination to another, while others leave the mainline churches for the African Initiative or Pentecostal churches. They may leave for a number of reasons: the mainline churches are too westernized, too cold spiritually, lack an emphasis on spiritual gifts (hence many members go to the so-called "prophets"), or hold to a liturgy that is completely foreign.

Fifth, the North African churches were probably the first Latin-speaking churches of the world. Again, it is possible that the first translations of the scriptures into Latin were made in North Africa. The great Latin Christian leaders, such as Tertullian (c. 160–220) and Cyprian (200–258), produced splendid Latin literature, later to be overshadowed by the towering achievements of Augustine of Hippo (354–430).[70] However, the North Africa church was absolutely Latinized, to the extent that it abandoned the indigenous languages, and produced great leaders such as Augustine, a Libyan Berber who grew up two hundred miles from the sea, was educated at Carthage, and "spoke no language other than Latin."[71] Roland Bainton observed that North Africa's renouncing of the old Punic and Berber elements in the church might have led to the indigenous people's rejection, not just of Rome as their colonizer, but also of Christianity, which was associated with the latter.[72]

One only hopes that after being colonized by the British, the French, and the Portuguese, the church in Africa will not keep on promoting colonial cultures alone; we also need to promote our vernacular languages and thought forms. Studies of African cultures, African religion, and vernacular languages are rich sources of African thought forms, proverbs, and idioms. Christianity in sub-Sahara Africa needs to be *de-europeanized* and *de-americanized*, especially in the areas of liturgy, styles of preaching, and church administration.

Chapter 3

Evangelizing Ethiopia

The country of Ethiopia is a mountainous kingdom once known as Abyssinia. It is considered the oldest independent African nation; its independence goes back to Biblical times.[73] Ethiopia is mentioned in several Biblical texts as *Kush*.

Meroitic Civilization

It is important to note that the whole region south of Egypt was known as *Kush* or Ethiopia. This means that the eunuch or the minister of finance identified as Ethiopian in Acts 8:27–28 might actually have come from the kingdom of Meroe, in what is now northern Sudan. Meroe flourished from 300 BCE until 350 CE, when the growing kingdom of Askum in Ethiopia proper finally conquered it. The basic mindset and motivation of Meroitic civilization was that of ancient Egypt. The kings called themselves the kings of Upper and Lower Egypt and the Egyptian gods were worshipped in the temples of Meroe; their kings lived the high-priestly life of Egyptian Pharaohs. They led their people in the ceremonies of seedtime and harvest. By the first century CE, the Meroitic civilization was already on the decline.[74] However, the above explanation should not rule out the possibility that the eunuch came from Askum, which was the growing power in Ethiopia proper.

Origin of Christianity in Ethiopia

Libya and Egypt are the African countries mentioned in the story of the day of Pentecost as having citizens present in Jerusalem (Acts 2:10). However, Sindima quotes John Chrysostom from his Epiphany homily as saying "the Ethiopian also understood,"[75] meaning that Ethiopians were also present in Jerusalem on the day of Pentecost. Nevertheless, as with those who came from Egypt and Libya, we have no information that they were responsible for bringing Christianity to Ethiopia. Tradition has it, however, that the apostles Matthew and Thomas preached the gospel in Ethiopia, and that Matthew was martyred in Ethiopia.[76] This tradition of Matthew and Thomas having preached in Ethiopia is debatable concerning its accuracy.

Luke, a companion and colleague of Paul, who authored both the Gospel According to Saint Luke and the Acts of the Apostles in the 70s or 80s CE, proved to be the first historian of the early church. He was a native of Antioch and a physician (Col. 4:14). Luke himself is said to have "died unmarried and childless in Boeotia at the age of eighty-four."[77] He left Africa a beautiful and informative story about one of the earliest baptized African Christians—an Ethiopian eunuch, court official of the queen of Ethiopia, minister of finance in charge of her entire treasury (Acts 8:27). The eunuch, a "God-fearer"[78] in Luke's parlance, received baptism by Philip the evangelist while passing through Samaria on his return journey to Ethiopia from Jerusalem where he had gone to worship (Acts 8:26–40).

The story of the Ethiopian suggests that Christianity may have reached Africa in the first century. Eusebius supported this view and exhorted that it came about for the purpose of fulfilling the prophecy, "Ethiopia shall stretch out her hand to God (Ps. 68:31)."[79] Origen (185–254) is quoted as saying, "The Gospel is not said to have been preached to all the Ethiopians, especially to such as live beyond the river,"[80] implying Christianity was indeed preached in Ethiopia during or before his time. Taken together, these references confirm as historical fact that Christian communities could have been found in Ethiopia, particularly in Askum, as early as the first and second centuries CE.

Frumentius and Edesius

In ancient times, traveling merchants or pupils in search of a mentor commonly crossed borders from one country to another. Thus, known records about the evangelization of Ethiopia are associated with a Syrian young man, Frumentius, in the early fourth century. The story is that a Syrian merchant or a Christian philosopher from Tyre, named Meropius, sailed down the Red Sea on a tour of exploration, possibly to India. Meropius took with him two young Syrian nephews, Edesius and Frumentius. On their return trip, their ship stopped at an Ethiopian port for water and the whole crew was massacred, but the two young men survived. It may have been because of their young age or purely the providence of God that they were spared. The two young men were taken to the King of Ethiopia, Ella Amida, at Aksum, the capital of Ethiopia then. The king seemed to have had a liking for and confidence in the two young men. He made Edesius his cup-bearer, and made Frumentius either the keeper of records or administrator of finances. Having been seized by the desire to know about Christians nearby, and to establish a Christian community, Frumentius was granted permission to explore as well as to propagate the new faith. He began leading worship services and was able to lead many people to the Christian faith.

The king died, leaving Ezana the prince as an infant. Frumentius acted as regent, and was also able to lead the prince to Christ. When the prince came of age and became fully in charge over his inheritance, the two Syrian men asked for permission to return to Syria, their homeland. The prince granted them permission. They traveled down the Nile River, and upon reaching Egypt, Frumentius decided to contact Bishop Athanasisus. Aedesius returned to Tyre, leaving Frumentius in Alexandria. In contacting Bishop Athanasius, Frumentius's idea was to beg the bishop to send missionaries to Askum as he had found the people there ready to receive the new faith; he also wanted to share the existence and needs of the church in the Ethiopian capital, Aksum. Athanasius received him warmly, and he agreed that the need was urgent. Realizing Frumentius was already fluent in the language of the people in Ethiopia, he ordained and consecrated Frumentius the first *Abuna* or bishop of the Ethiopian Orthodox Church. Athanasius sent him back to Aksum in 330 CE, accompanied by some missionaries.[81]

The propagation of the gospel under the preaching of Frumentius is said to have been successful, for he touched not only the Abyssinians, but also the Blemmyes and Nubians.[82] Tradition has it that "Frumentius with zealous foresight translated the New Testament into Ethiopic or *Ghiz*."[83] Frumentius was later called *Abba Salama*, meaning Father of Light,[84] and also, *Abuna Salama* or Bishop of Peace. Another group of Egyptian monks was sent to Ethiopia about 480 CE.[85]

Since the time of Athanasius, the Patriarch of Alexandria appointed all succeeding Abunas of the Ethiopian Church, but the practice stopped in the twentieth century. Further, because all the Abunas were appointed by Alexandria, they were therefore from the Coptic Church and Egyptian by nationality. In October 1951, Debra Libanos, an Ethiopian primate, was installed as the first Ethiopian Abuna in Cairo.[86]

Nine Saints from Syria

The fourth and fifth centuries were characterized by Christological controversies that affected many churches negatively, especially in the eastern area of the Roman Empire. The church in the West (of the Roman Empire) favoured the teaching that Jesus Christ had two natures—one divine and the other human. The church in the East, which had Hellenistic orientation, favoured a Christology that stated that the divine and human natures of Christ were fused into a single nature at his birth. We have already noted that when the Ecumenical Council of Chalcedon (451) decided in favour of the West, that decision put the eastern Christian communities in disarray.

In following their Christological persuasion, we noted earlier that the eastern churches ended up with a Christology known as *monophysicism*. Those Christological controversies for quite some time had great affect on relationships between regions and Christian communities, with bishops accusing one another, and several of them losing their Sees, although some regained them. It is said there exists a letter from the Arian Emperor, Constantius, to the King of Aksum urging him to obtain his bishop from Arian sources rather than from Athanasius, "who is guilty of ten thousand crimes."[87]

Indeed, there were some Syrian missionaries, whom Ethiopia remembers as the Nine Saints, who arrived in the fifth century CE. They established monasteries and translated the Bible into *Ge'ez* from a version of the Septuagint in use in the Patriarchate of Antioch. It is possible, but not certain, that they were *monophysites*, possibly fleeing from the aftermath of the Chalcedon decision. From that time on, the Ethiopian Church espoused the *monophysite* cause with passionate conviction. Increasingly, Ethiopian Christianity became noticeably influenced by Byzantium (Constantinople).[88]

The Solomonic Tradition

The royal house of Ethiopia was founded on the supposition that it descended from Menelik, the son of Solomon and the Queen of Sheba. The story is that after the Queen of Sheba visited Solomon, upon her return home, she bore him a child, Menelik. The son grew up to be called Menelik I of Askum. Menelik is alleged to have returned to Jerusalem, taken the Ark, and brought it to Ethiopia to his own people. Therefore, there developed a dynasty of Menelik, for later on there was Menelik II. In the course of time, the "*Solomonic* tradition became the core symbol of Christian Ethiopia, the cornerstone of its sense of national identity."[89] That relationship of Ethiopian Christianity with the Solomonic tradition brought Jewish if not Hebraic practices, undiluted by Hellenistic thought forms, into the life and especially the liturgy of the Ethiopian church.[90]

By the ninth century CE, Askum was on the decline. In the twelfth century, Ethiopia was under the leadership of the Zagwe dynasty, which came from central Ethiopia and made great religious achievements. Their king, named Lalibela, made ten church buildings carved out of the living rock, deserving to be one of the wonders of the world. Later on, the dynasty was challenged for "not being of the pure *Solomonid* lineage—that is not being descended from Menelik, a son of Solomon and the Queen of Sheba, who supposedly founded the royal house of Ethiopia."[91]

Ethiopia, according to reports, became a land of churches and church buildings. A distinctive Ethiopian style of religious architecture and worship evolved that is evident today. The architecture of the village church buildings is round or octagonal, with a conical grass roof. Chanting and drumming mark worship in the round sanctuaries. This uniqueness of Ethiopian Christianity, though considered by many as secretive or mysterious, is what makes it unique.

Islam in Ethiopia

Muslim conquest in Egypt in the seventh century cut off the Christian community in Ethiopia, not only from Egypt but also from the rest of Christendom. Ethiopian Christianity went into deep isolation. Nevertheless, because of its mountain outpost, Islam was never able to effectively overcome the Christian culture in spite of many attempts to do so.[92] From the time of Arabic conquest in Egypt and North Africa, Ethiopia maintained links with the outside world in two ways. One linkage was an Ethiopian monastery in Jerusalem, which remained an important pilgrimage site for pious monks from Ethiopia. Another was the Coptic Patriarch in Alexandria who continued to supply the Ethiopian Church its *Abuna*. In the course of history, Christians and Muslims in Ethiopia agreed not to fight each other. That enabled the Ethiopian church to maintain its independence, culture, identity, and faith.

Summary

Here are a few observations about how Ethiopia was evangelized and how the brand of Ethiopian Christianity developed.

First, the stories of the eunuch, who was minister of finance from Ethiopia, and of Matthew and Thomas, who preached in Ethiopia, forge an interesting linkage of Ethiopian Christianity with the early church of Jerusalem.

Second, the Ethiopian brand of Christianity was influenced by a number of quarters: (a) Originally, Alexandrian Christianity influenced it, then the Coptic Church of Egypt, which continued to appoint the *Abuna* for the Ethiopian Orthodox Church until the twentieth century. (b) Syrian influence was also fairly strong, including Frumentius, the first *Abuna*, and the Nine Saints from Syria, who established monasteries and translated the scriptures into Geez. (c) Evidence of Arabic influence is evident in the ancient Ethiopic language, Geez, still the liturgical language of the Ethiopian Orthodox Church, which is derived from the ancient Serbian tongue of Southern Arabia. (d) The royal house of Ethiopia was founded on the supposition that it descended from Menelik, the son of Solomon and the Queen of Sheba.

Third, it is noteworthy that the Ethiopian Orthodox Church seems not to have exerted any external influence directly, "nor taken part in any extension of the Christian faith to the rest of the continent."[93]

Fourth, the Ethiopian nation and the Ethiopian Orthodox Church have exerted some influence "mysteriously," in spite of the Ethiopian Church not being evangelical. The fact that the Ethiopian Orthodox Church absorbed all those different influences from different sources, and the nation was not colonized and became so proud of its independence, enabled the church to brew its own brand of Christianity, even to formulate its own type of liturgy and church architecture. Isichei says, "Christian Ethiopia, like the Coptic community, is not a mission field at all; it was an ancient and thoroughly *Africanized* church that would have provided most valuable precedents for other African Christians, had they come into contact with it."[94] Beginning in the 1920s, western missionaries in sub-Saharan Africa feared the encroachment of Islam southward and feared the Ethiopian brand of Christianity, which some of their authors termed *Ethiopianism*.

Now that we are increasingly making contact with Ethiopian

Christianity, we know about their churches carved in stone, the round or octagon shaped church buildings, and all that other churches can learn from Ethiopia. There is a need to move away from the Roman *basilica* style architecture of church buildings that at times look so strange in African villages of round houses. Round houses are beautiful, too. The Africa University campus is beautifully arranged in a semi-circle to reflect that design, with the University Chapel also designed in an octagon shape at the end of the semi-circle.

Fifth, Ethiopian Christianity needs to be understood in light of African religion, where religion is taken as a way of life without *proselytizing*.[95] This explains its lack of evangelical zeal or mission to the other regions of Africa. Be that as it may, from the beginning of the twentieth century, the history of the Ethiopian church and of the Ethiopians as a people raised political awareness and inspired struggle for liberation, hence, the missionaries coining the term E*thiopianism*. This led to the mushrooming of independent churches especially in Southern Africa, and the desire for attachment to the continent by Blacks in the Diaspora, for example, the R*astafarians* who were inspired by Haile Selassie. No wonder Addis Ababa became the headquarters of the Organization of African Unity (1963–2002) and now the African Union since 2002.

Chapter 4

Evangelizing the Kongo Kingdom

Sub-Saharan Africa remained unknown to Europe until the fifteenth century CE, when Henry, a prince of Portugal, popularly known as Henry the Navigator (1394 – 1460) opened the way. He had interest in the sea, so he built a small castle and tower near a place called Sagres, on the southern coast of Portugal. He invited many explorers, mapmakers, geographers, and sea captains from all over Europe to come to his castle to study and exchange ideas and information.[96]

Henry began the exploration of Africa, but first with the desire to discover the real strength of the Moors, who had conquered Spain and Portugal in the eighth century CE. His broader purpose for promoting African discovery was fivefold: (a) to extend geographical knowledge; (b) to extend Portuguese trade; (c) to discover the real strength of the Moors[97]; (d) to see whether he might find any Christian prince who could become an ally against the Moors; (e) and finally, "to make increase in the faith of our Lord Jesus Christ and to bring to him all the souls that should be saved."[98]

Henry's people entered Ceuta,[99] a city now in Morocco. He used Ceuta as a springboard from which he made expeditions further on the coast of West Africa. In 1482, the Portuguese landed at Elmina, Ghana. In Nigeria, the King of Benin received missionaries from Portugal, not because he wanted missionaries, but arms. Thus, six years later the King of Benin was baptized.

Christianity in West Africa

In 1655, Spanish Friars visited Benin and Sierra Leone. A Father Barrerius won over to Christianity a chief of Sierra Leone at the beginning of the seventeenth century. In order for the chief to qualify for baptism, he had to divorce all his wives, except one. He was baptized and given the name Philip, after Philip II of Spain. Although the Roman Catholics meant to evangelize the people on the coast of West Africa, their work was not long-lasting. The motivation for conversion was unable to produce in the convert any permanent change of life.

Until 1617, Roman Catholics carried on Christian activities in West Africa. But in 1618, Protestants began coming into West Africa, beginning with the English who built two forts along the coast located in the Gambia, and another at Cormantine in Gold Coast in the same year. The Dutch entered Gold Cost in 1637 and captured the Portuguese forts along the coast, including Elmina. Later, the French, Danes, Swedes, and Brandenburgers also established themselves on the coast. They built their forts to serve the commercial and spiritual welfare of the occupants. Each fort was afforded a chaplain to care for the spiritual welfare of the Europeans. The chaplain played an essential part in the fort's daily routine, and held a high position—always close to the governor or director-general.

There were problems establishing Christianity in West Africa during that time. The Dutch, Danes, and English sent young West Africans to their European homelands to study and to return as priests in their respective churches. At times the results were not good; some failed to readjust; others even forgot their mother language. The immoral life of Europeans in West Africa, who at the same time professed the Christian faith, created another barrier. Finally, in spite of their efforts to introduce Christianity to West Africa, these groups established no permanent mission stations.[100]

In the thirteenth century, Portugal and Spain emerged as the two most powerful nations, and struggled for control of the new lands that were being discovered by the Europeans. In 1493, the Pope issued the Bill of Demarcation, which proclaimed that all lands west of a line passing the

Azores belonged to Spain, while all new discoveries to the east were to become the rightful property of Portugal.[101] The division of the new lands between the two powers came in the wake of several explorers who had crossed oceans to discover such new lands. Through the efforts of Prince Henry the Navigator's mariners, Bartholomew Diaz (1450–1500) was able to round the Southern tip of Africa in 1486.[102] Vasco da Gama (1469–1524) followed with another exploration, reaching the Cape of Good Hope in 1497.[103]

Often, the western powers launched political expansion and evangelization side by side. Therefore, in these explorations of the African coasts, priests accompanied the expeditions and served as chaplains to the new trading settlements and as missionaries to neighbouring African peoples.[104]

Christianity in the Kingdom of Kongo

In 1482 the Portuguese came into contact with one of the most powerful Bantu Kingdoms of Africa, the Kingdom of the Kongo.[105] The name of the king was *Manikongo*, and "its capital *Mbanzakongo*, the modern Sao Salvador in northern Angola."[106] Portugal's objective in coming to West Africa was to bring Christianity and higher civilization or "Christian civilization" to Africa. In order to achieve their plan's objectives, the Portuguese government authorities worked hand in hand with the church. The Portuguese priests penetrated several villages and built churches and schools. Actually, it was in West Central Africa that "the first real attempts at colonial control were made by conversion to Christianity and establishment of the Kingdom as a vassal of the Portuguese Crown."[107] Therefore, in 1490, missionaries consisting of builders, carpenters, and many others with different skills were sent to the Kongo Kingdom from Portugal.[108] *Manikongo* himself and several of his chiefs and family members converted and were baptized. The capital was rebuilt with stone. Many young people were sent to Europe for education. It is said that while the earlier converts might not have been serious about their new faith, Nzinga Mbemba, who was baptized as Afonso in 1491,[109] succeeded to the throne in 1505 and ruled as a determined Christian king until his death in 1543. He would have remodeled his kingdom along the lines of those of Western Europe had it not been for the issue of slave trade.

Little did the Kongo kings know that the Portuguese had a hidden agenda beyond bringing Christianity to West Africa! The Portuguese planned "to change the Blacks into the white man's image—a process ... which caused the Blacks to reject and become ashamed of both their culture and themselves."[110] This system was understood in many quarters as *assimilado*—"a civilizing mission." Even by 1950, four centuries after the civilizing mission began, less than one per cent of Africans in Angola qualified for citizenship status in their own country.[111] In fact, the system was actually for both Christianizing and civilizing the African. Most missionaries from Europe, America, Australia, New Zealand, and other places used some form of this approach to evangelize sub-Saharan Africa. The differences were a matter of degree.

Christianity for Slave Trade

Because of that twofold process of Christianizing and civilizing the Africans, the Portuguese plan in the Kongo used missionaries to lead the way in working "on the kings and then their councilors." That created the appropriate atmosphere to introduce Jesuit Fathers to be installed as councilors to the king, one of them even functioning as a prime minister.[112] The kings were now making decisions without referring matters to their traditional councilors. The result was that the kings tended to become absolute monarchs in the hands of the white Portuguese. Also, the "idea of divine kingship was promoted through the anointment and crowning of kings by Portuguese bishops. Kings now ruled as "sons of the Church," chosen by divine decree to serve it. This meant serving the Portuguese by meeting their demands—always made as friendly suggestions from brothers who were "equal in Christ."[113]

Increasingly, Kongolese kings lost touch with their culture and tradition as well as their people. A good number of them, such as Alvares, Dom Pedros, Diogos became known as "Black Portuguese."[114] Chancellor Williams wrote, "They lost their history, so they died." That has been one of the tragedies of African Christianity.

When Afonso became king, it eventually became clear the Portuguese's plan was to make Africans into slaves, not Christians. Some of the young African men were sent to study in Portugal. Afonso's son, Henrique, after thirteen years of study in Portugal, returned to the Kongo as bishop, not of Kongo, but as titular bishop of a Muslim province in North Africa. When the Portuguese clergy marginalized him, he became depressed and ill. Henrique went to Europe in 1529, and died on a return voyage in the 1530s.[115]

There is no doubt that initially the African kings and the people of Kongo believed the Portuguese were introducing them to a better life. Afonso sent requests to Portugal "for what we would now call development aid, and stone masons, 'two physicians and two apothecaries and one surgeon', and many other things were sent."[116] However, Portugal needed slaves for the plantations in Brazil. At first, Afonso was prepared to pay for imports with slaves, until later he realized that the price was too high.[117] For the Portuguese colonialists, however, there was no point of return; Afonso had to keep supplying slaves.

Afonso realised that the Portuguese had come to his country more for slaves than for the introduction of the new religion and to bring a better life for his people. Some of the Portuguese clergy became "involved in trade, including slave trade, and often at odds with each other."[118] Afonso wrote to Portugal, complaining:

> ...our country is being completely depopulated, and Your Highness should not agree with this norm accept it as in your service. And to avoid it we need from those (your) Kingdoms no more than some priests and a few people to

> teach in schools, and no other goods accept wine and flour for the holy sacraments.[119]

All these complaints fell on deaf ears. As a matter of fact, at the instigation of a friar, a group of Portuguese attempted to assassinate Afonso at the Easter service of 1540.[120] In spite of those attempts, Afonso remained Christian.[121] He ruled until his death in 1543.[122]

Finally, due to the intensive efforts of the Portuguese to capture the African people for slaves for their plantations in Brazil, all efforts to establish Christianity in the Kingdom of Kongo then collapsed. From then on, the Kongolese had to grapple with the rising force of this foreign culture that had been introduced into the country. Although the Kongo became a see in 1596, with the king of Portugal appointing a Portuguese bishop, few Kongolese were ordained.[123] The situation had drastically changed. The Kongolese kings felt Portugal had betrayed them. To make things worse, forces coming out of Luanda, Angola, invaded the Kingdom of Kongo. That was the end of Portuguese efforts to evangelize Africa.

Summary

We can make several observations about Portugal's attempt to bring Christianity and higher civilization, or "Christian civilization," to West Central Africa.

First, the Portuguese efforts to bring Christianity to the Kongo Kingdom in the fifteenth century CE turned into an enterprise in slave trade. This is an issue often cited by some African politicians who choose to speak against the church or against the missionaries. Christians, especially our Christian leaders, need to understand that the Portuguese abuse of Christianity in the Kongo Kingdom in the fifteenth century is a fact. And it was repeated elsewhere later, though to different degrees. Nevertheless, the criticism of missionaries should not be overly generalized.

Second, Portuguese Christianity in the Kongo Kingdom used and emphasized the concept of conversion to mean *Europeanizing* or

Portuguezizing the Africans, i.e., making the African Christians abandon their African culture and adopt the Portuguese way of life. That process was known as the policy of *assimilado*, which was a negation of indigenization. Let it be noted, however, that not only the Portuguese but also the missionaries of other church traditions failed to grasp Paul's theology of "the freedom that we have in Christ Jesus" (Gal. 2:4), who also acted like "Judaizers." One result was that African converts who picked up European and American names as their vernacular names were condemned. We need to recognize that this was not merely a problem with the missionaries, who are long gone; many of us African church leaders today cannot entirely extricate ourselves from the missionary mentality.

A preacher told a story of a farmer whose cattle refused to eat dray and brown grass at the end of the rainy season, after being accustomed to seeing green grass. So the farmer goggled the cattle with green spectacles, making them see green objects once more. When he put the same old dry and brown grass before them, to his delight they started eating because the grass looked green. As African leaders, we need to remove the missionary spectacles of the eighteenth and nineteenth centuries; we need to see the church in Africa through African eyes.

Third, some women prophets emerged in an effort to contextualize Portuguese Christianity in West Central Africa during those difficult days. Two such African women were *Appolonia Mafuta* and *Vita Kimpa*. The latter was a young woman baptized as Beatrice who claimed to be the medium of St. Antony. She belonged to the nobility, and had been a *n'anga*, i.e. a traditional healer and herbalist or a diviner. She taught that Jesus had been born in the Kongo capital, and that he was black. She was burnt at the stake for heresy in 1706 at the age of twenty.[124] The elder *Appolonia Mafuta* who supported *Vita Kimpaher's* ministry was trying to understand Jesus Christ in the African context. She had the courage to remove the western green spectacles and begin the process of looking at her Master as an African through African eyes.

Chapter 5

European Scramble for Africa

Prior to the time when the missionary societies sent missionaries to evangelize Africa beginning in the nineteenth century, other groups of European origin had already come to Africa—slave traders, explorers, and colonialists. Although those European groups came to Africa independently and separately, there is a sense in which they were all connected, as the coming of one group opened the door for the other. One could also say that because of a colonial scramble for Africa, some missionary societies joined the bandwagon. We need to understand, however, the separateness as well as the relatedness of those European groups, and especially their relationship to missionary groups. Further, we need to understand their roles and the impact they made on African life, because the evangelization of the rest of sub-Saharan Africa took place in such historical and transitional context.

Slave Trade and Slavery

At the outset, let us be clear that before the coming of the Europeans, some parts of Africa already practiced slavery of those who were captured at war. In some African communities they killed the warriors of a conquered ethnic group, but often integrated the innocent. Women of the conquered group were often taken into marriage and the young people were incorporated into the ethnic group of the conquerors. What was new after the coming of the Europeans was the introduction of training and arming bands of African allies to make war on the peoples in the surrounding villages—burning their homes and capturing them in order to select those who were to be exported as slaves.

Slave trade began and thrived in the coastal countries of West Africa. The Dutch, who had pushed the Portuguese from Ghana in 1642, are said to have been the pioneers of exporting African slaves from Ghana.[125] The other European nations followed suit: France in Senegal-Gambia, Britain in Ghana and Niger Delta, and of course the Portuguese in the Kongo and Mozambique.

European slave traders bought slaves from the African chiefs living close to the coast who had developed a taste for European imports such as cloth, hardware and metals, spirits, and firearms.[126] Oliver and Page estimate that by the end of the sixteenth century 275,000 slaves had landed overseas. By the seventeenth century, the number was 1,340,000; by the eighteenth century, 6,050,000; and by the nineteenth century, 11,900,000.[127]

In chapter 4, we discussed how the Portuguese in the fifteenth century opted for slave trade instead of evangelizing the Kongo Kingdom. Portugal and Spain, the two superpowers of the time, tried to use Indians as labour in the New World, but found the system unsatisfactory. In 1517, Charles I of Spain (Charles V, Holy Roman Emperor) "disregarding papal disapproval, granted letters patent to Spanish settlers to import African slaves into the Caribbean islands (Cuba, Haiti, Puerto Rico, and others) and later to the main land."[128] In Brazil, where sugar cane and coffee were cultivated, the Portuguese started with a few African slaves that soon became a flood. A Dutch vessel was the first to export slaves to Virginia in northern America. There the trade was slower; they had about 2,000 slaves in Virginia in 1681, 59,000 in 1714, and 263,000 by 1754. Due to the introduction of cotton in the southern United States, there were 4.5 million slaves by 1860.[129] To supply the Caribbean islands and mainland America with slaves, the rest of Europe got involved in the slave trade. Liverpool, Bristol, and other western ports dominated.[130] In that slave trade, there developed what came to be known as the triangular trade in the Atlantic.

> To the Slave Coast of Guinea home ports in Europe came liquor, arms, piece goods and trinkets with which captains of ships purchased slaves, who were then carried across the ocean closely and cruelly packed; some 20% died on the way. In the Americas the ships reloaded with rum, tobacco and other local products. [131]

In North America, as in the Cape of South Africa, a distorted Calvinistic theology equated white immigrants with Israelites and black slaves with Canaanites, "hewers of wood and drawers of water." Historians estimate that before the onset of the nineteenth century, more Africans had crossed the Atlantic than European colonialists, and that in the Americas slaves numbered not less that fifteen million.[132]

As people learned more about the horrors of slave trade and slavery, the anti-slavery movement developed. It happened that the Protestant churches of Germany, Britain, and the American colonies (now USA) experienced evangelical revivals. These revivals stressed people's need to have a personal conversion to Christ, and that began to bring change within the churches themselves. Both the evangelical movement and the Quakers (or Religious Society of Friends) developed a new conscience about slavery. There is a sense in which the moral conscience that arose within the evangelical movement gave birth to the anti-slavery movement and crusade. The evangelical movement also gave birth to Protestant missionary efforts.

One of the greatest changes that took place between 1750 and 1850 was the change from acceptance and support of slavery to verbal, legal, and military attacks on slavery. The first stage of this vast change in Western Christianity came with a moral awakening among Quakers in America. In 1688, the Quaker society in Germantown, Pennsylvania, made the first protest. However, it was John Woolman (1720–72) and others who organized and spread accurate information about slavery. This made it possible for others to wake up to what was happening and to affect change. As early as 1761, all Quakers engaged in the slave trade were disowned (excommunicated) by the Society.

One of the most important converts to anti-slavery was John Wesley, the English evangelical preacher. In 1772 he read a book by an American Quaker and turned against slavery, preaching continuously against it. In Britain, a political battle to destroy slavery and the slave trade was waged. That battle was accompanied by a philanthropic effort to build something better than slave trading in Africa. A group of British evangelicals called the Clapham Sect was most active in this effort.

After the freeing of slaves in Britain, a movement grew to return the slaves to Africa. This was the beginning of the colonization of Sierra Leone from Britain, and then later of Liberia from America. The idea of the Sierra Leone colony was not all humanitarian. For most people, it was a way for Britain to get rid of undesirable people, like the Negro ex-slaves. But some Christians became influential in the direction this enterprise took. By 1834, slavery was abolished in the British Empire. Ex-slaves from Britain and its colonies were re-settled in Sierra Leone, and many from America resettled in Liberia. We must note that ultimately the League of Nations, which was formed in 1920, outlawed slavery, as did the United Nations, which was formed in 1945.[133]

European Explorers on the Continent

The second group in the European scramble for Africa after slave traders was the European explorers. The interior of the African continent was still unknown to the Europeans. From the fifteenth century, several European ships had sailed along the coast and around Africa, especially the Cape of Good Hope, to and from the east, without penetrating the continent itself. The captains of slave trade ships often remained at the coast while someone else penetrated the interior to vandalize and capture the slaves for them. They too, however, never penetrated the forests of Africa.

Initially, the European explorers explored the African rivers, with particular interest in establishing their sources and the direction in which they flowed to the ocean. These explorers from Britain, France, and Germany started to penetrate the forests of Africa. The Association for Promoting the Discovery of the Interior Parts of Africa (commonly known as the African Association), founded in 1788, had its French counterpart in Napoleon's Expedition *d'Egypte* (1798–1801).[134] However, records of earlier discovery expeditions had come from Portuguese sources. Giovanni Battista's *Ramusio's Delle Navigationi e Viaggi* (Venice, 1550) describes a Portuguese embassy to Ethiopia in 1520. Also, a Portuguese Dominican named Joao de los Santos, in his *Ethiopia Oriental* (1607), exceeds the scope of his title by providing a brilliant survey of the eastern coast of Africa as far as Mozambique. "By contrast, two later French writers, *Guillaume Delisle* (1675–1726) and Jean-Batiste *Bourguignon d'Anville* (1697–1782) exhibit profound ignorance, even, making the Niger flow east from Lake Chad."[135]

Geographical or scientific societies like the African Association often sponsored individual explorers, including missionary minded personalities, to increase their knowledge of Africa. Such societies would cite their interests in those expeditions as: (a) attacking the slave trade, (b) seeking to introduce legitimate commerce, and, (c) seeking to introduce Christianity. Some of the rivers, lakes, and mountains that they explored included these:

The Nile River. James Bruce, a Scot, went to Ethiopia in 1768, "and saw the source of the Blue Nile."[136] In the process, he was welcomed "to the Ethiopian capital of Gondar or to that of the Funj Kingdom at Sennar on the Blue Nile."[137]

The Upper Niger. The African Association financed the exploration Mungo Park's journey to the Upper Niger in 1795–97. Park returned to the same place in 1805–06.[138] It is important to note that Sir Joseph Banks and Sir John Barrow succeeded in implanting in the British government the idea that exploration was a proper subject for official expenditure. It was in British government pay that Park returned to Africa to sail down most of the course of the Niger in 1806; that Denham and Clapperton explored Bornu and Hausaland after crossing the Sahara from Tripoli during 1823–25; that the Landen brothers traced the course of the lower Niger to the sea in 1830; and that the great German explorer Heinrich Barth undertook his meticulous explorations in the Central and Western Sudan during 1850–55.[139]

Kilimanjaro and Mt. *Kenya*. In 1847–49, two German members of the Church Missionary Society (CMS), Johann Ludwig Krapt and Johannes Rebmann, were the first Europeans "to see the snow-capped peaks of Kilimanjaro and Mt. Kenya."[140] The journeys of Krapt and Rebmann were primarily missionary in intent, as were David Livingstone's early journeys.[141]

Lake Chad. German explorer Gerhard Rohlts made extensive journeys in North Africa Sahara, a job that was later extended by other Germans, "notably Gustav Nachtigal, who in 1870–74 explored the Sudan between Lake Chad and the Nile."[142]

Monomotapas. Karl Mauch, between 1860–72, was the first European in modern times to explore the region of the ancient Monomotapas in Zimbabwe.

The Gambia River. Gaspard-Theodore Mollien, a French naval officer, visited Futa Jallon on donkey-back, when he saw the source of the Gambia and other rivers in 1818.[143]

Victoria Falls. Missionary David Livingstone traveled overland from the south to the Victoria Falls 1853–56, and "thence westwards to Luanda and eastwards again to the mouth of the Zambezi."[144] Having published his travels under the title *Missionary Travels and Researches*, Livingstone "aroused the enthusiasm of Victorian England for the opening of this side of the continent to Christianity and Commerce."[145] The African Association, which by then had developed into the powerful Royal Geographical Society and received government subsidy, supported Livingstone's travels.[146] It was the same society that sponsored Livingstone's exploration to the Zambezi in 1859–64, in the course of which he saw Lake Malawi. Because he had become rich from the sale of his book, he sponsored himself to explore "the upper reaches of the Congo in 1867–73."[147] Livingstone's work was popularized by the visit of H. M. Stanley, a journalist who left America to look up Livingstone in the heart of Africa. The famous phrase, "Dr. Livingstone, I presume," is Stanley's.[148]

Lake Tanganyika and Victoria Nyanza. Burton and Speke traveled to Lake Tanganyika in 1858, and Speke and Grant to the Victoria Nyanza and down the Nile in 1867–74. The Royal Geographical Society sponsored them all.[149]

The Congo. H. M. Stanley's work had tremendous impact on Europe and America. King Leopold of the Belgians had interest in the Congo. One can easily see how Christianity and colonialism came to Africa as twin sisters. For example, David Livingstone's aim as a missionary and a geographer was to open up commerce to make a road for Christianity in Africa. For the Brussels International Geographical Conference of 1884, the aim was to plant the flag of civilization on the soil of Central Africa to combat the slave trade.

Colonists and the Partitioning of the Land

The exploration of Africa's interior in the nineteenth century eventually led to a European scramble for African colonies. The first European power in the scramble for Africa was King Leopold II, not representing Belgium as much as his own personal interest. Having succeeded to the throne in 1865, he encouraged exploration of central Africa. By 1876, he had founded a chain of commercial and scientific stations from Zanzibar to the Atlantic. "The stations were to be garrisoned, and they were to serve as bases from which to attack slave trade and to protect Christian missions."[150] The first two explorations entered through East Africa in 1878 and 1879, and attached themselves to mission stations of the White Fathers at Tabora and Lake Tanganyika.[151] Taking advantage of H. M. Stanley's trip down the Congo River in 1877, King Leopold used Stanley to open up the Congo for him in 1879. He operated water transport from the mouth of the Congo River to modern Kisangani, more than a thousand miles away. He prepared "for international recognition of his rule over the whole area of the Congo basin."[152] His real intention was to develop the Congo basin "as a free-trade area under his 'international' regime" rather than let it fall to any other national rivals.[153] Many believe Leopold, more than any other statesman, created the scrambling for colonies.[154]

Germany was the next power to penetrate Africa between 1883 and 1885. The Germans moved into Southwest Africa, Togoland, Cameroon, and East Africa. Britain was already in Africa by 1879—in Gambia, Sierra Leone, Gold Coast, Lagos, and Cape Colony. France was in Africa by 1879—in Algeria, Senegal, Gabon, and East Africa. Portugal, the earliest colonial power in Africa, was in Angola and Mozambique by 1879.

British and French roles in the scramble for Africa are important to understand. "In 1881, the joint Anglo-French financial control had broken down in face of the revolt of the national army, led by one of its most senior Egyptian Officers, Urabi Pasha."[155] In order to crush the revolt, the British and the French planned to act jointly. On the eve of the attack, something prevented the French from joining Britain. Britain crushed the revolt alone, and occupied Egypt until it became a protectorate in 1914. The Britons refused to allow France to come in after they crushed the revolt, so France shifted their attention to West Africa, thus encouraging the spirit of the scramble. From then on, all of the European powers felt that they should have a piece of African land in their control, after which they drained the natural resources of mother Africa for the development of their own capitals. It was that scramble for Africa among the European powers that led to the Berlin Conference in December 1884.

Ethiopia was the only African country that remained unoccupied by a European power.

Summary

What observations can we make as we reflect upon the coming of the three European groups to Africa?

First, the events of slave trade and slavery, and the colonization of Africa, are historical events that brought trauma to the African people. That trauma affected not only the immediate victims of slave trade; it also affected those on the continent who escaped the slave trade, and the descendents of the victims of slave trade who now live in the African Diaspora.[156] People who have been hurt, and those who have hurt others even unintentionally, often find a way to come together, reconcile, and move forward. The story of Joseph and his brothers is helpful: "You intended to harm me, but God intended it for good to accomplish what is now being done, the saving of many lives" (Gen. 50:20). Today at African University students and staff take the whole month of February to celebrate with those in the Diaspora and to commemorate the Black History of the Africans in the Diaspora. What a glorious opportunity for promoting global togetherness!

Second, under the inspiration of leaders from the African Diaspora, a movement developed not only to defeat colonialism but also to recognize the oneness of all people on the African continent. Voices of such thinkers as Marcus Garvey and W. E. B. DuBois, as well as the ideas that flowed from the pan-African meetings, were significant. One such meeting at Manchester, England, in 1945, which was attended by African leaders from of the continent such as George Padmore, Kwame Nkrumah, and Jomo Kenyatta, became a benchmark. Africa is now facing a new era—a post-colonial era with new enemies. No one could have described this new post-colonial era better than did the Hon. Prime Minister Robert Gabriel Mugabe on 18 April 1980, Zimbabwe's Independence Day. In his message inviting the new nation to a mood and spirit of reconciliation, he said:

> As we become a new people, we are called to be constructive, progressive and forever forward looking, for we cannot afford to be men of yesterday...Our new nation requires everyone of us to be a new man with a new mind, a new heart and a

> new spirit that must unite and not divide. This is the human essence that must form the core of our political change and national independence. If yesterday I fought you as an enemy, today you have become a friend and ally with the same national interest.

That speech by the then-inaugurated Hon. Prime Minister of Zimbabwe marked the end of the old colonial era, and at the same time the dawn of the new era.

Third, in post-independent Africa a few of our nations have yet to deliver peace and development to their citizens. Instead, they have perpetuated traumatic experiences of torture and brutality through the use of police and the army. These governments have no respect for rule of law. Such regimes have established armies that are greatly equipped, as if the war with the colonialists was still going on. At a symposium convened by the All Africa Conferences of Churches (AACC), the statement of the collective church body observed that, because establishing and sustaining those African armies is so costly—an act that has impoverished our people—these nations "have not fought Africa's real enemies of poverty, insecurity, famine and illiteracy."[157] The symposium went on to state that the practice of barbarous acts currently carried out in the course of interrogations "or within prison walls, whether beatings, electric shocks, solitary confinement in cells with snakes, beasts or harmful insects and the detention of normal with mentally disturbed inmates…"[158] reduces human dignity, not only of the victim, but equally so of the victimizer. The result is that increasingly young people with skills are leaving their countries for greener pastures. African nations are again seriously robbed of their healthy bodied and skilled young men and women, this time not by slave trade, but by reckless regimes. And many, many unskilled young people of Africa are turned into bands of thieves and robbers in their own societies.

The church needs to continue communicating the message that every human being is created in the image of God and that human dignity must be preserved—that all human beings, without discrimination, must be accorded their basic human rights. Our message to leaders of such barbaric regimes is that in as much as some African leaders suffered terribly in the colonial jails, we need to teach our former masters that it is possible to treat one's political opponents humanely. Oh Africa! "But let justice roll on like a river, righteousness like a never-failing stream!" (Amos 5:24).

Chapter 6

Evangelizing the Rest of Sub-Saharan Africa

The evangelization of sub-Saharan Africa by the Protestant churches originated from a number of factors in Europe and later on in North America.

First, there was the rise of evangelical pietism in Europe and America. The word *piety* refers to personal faith and behaviour (see 1 Tim. 5:4, KJV) "which includes repentance and prayer and the practice of Christian love."[159] Piety is personal devotion to God, religious duties, and practices. Pietism, therefore, is "a system which stresses the devotional ideal in religion."[160] Simply stated, pietism is religion of the heart.

When Christianity acquired the status of a state religion in the fourth century, allowing more people to join the church without fear of persecution, and allowing more secular influence in the life of the church,[161] some Christians reacted by developing an ascetic or a monastic style of life—a style of pietism in the desert and the monastery. That ascetic or monastic life involved the practice of self-denial—choosing to leave worldly life and follow Christ in the company of the like-minded.[162] Similarly, from 1650 to 1800, a new society of secularism emerged in Europe and America, "in which religion was but one of the many interests."[163] As prelude to that period, Europe had been plunged into religious war, specifically the Thirty Years' War (1618–48), between the Roman Church and the Lutherans. It is said that about ten million of Germany's sixteen million people were killed.[164] By the end of thirty years of fighting, no one knew exactly why they were fighting. It was out of that experience of suffering by ordinary people, who roamed in the forests like animals, eating grass, at times even turning to cannibalism, that "in the wake of that struggle pietism, a vigorous evangelical reform emerged."[165]

Two of the prominent figures of evangelical pietism in Germany were Philipp Jakob Spener and August Hermann Frankle. Spener (1635–1705) was born thirteen years before the end of the Thirty Years' War. He knew something about the devastating results of the war, and longed for a change. Realizing how difficult it was going to be to exact reform through the formalized Lutheran State Church, Spener organized small groups that met in his home for Bible reading, prayer, and discussion.[166] In addition to a direct study of the Bible, he promoted the idea that having a right feeling in the heart was even more important than knowing pure doctrine.[167]

August Frankle (1663–1727) started a pietistic study group at the University of Leipzig in 1689. He was Spener's most famous disciple. Frankle left the University of Leipzig because of opposition and became a member of the newly established University of Halle. He built pietism into the teaching curriculum, training graduates and placing more than two hundred ministers each year in the German Church. He also heard and responded to the plight of the poor. He accomplished much: (a) The Protestant Church of Germany gained zealous ministers and layman. (b) Bible study became a common personal and group practice. (c) Devotional sincerity increased. (d) Social service spread, beginning with Frankle establishing a famous Orphan House at Halle in 1698. Many of its children became clergy, missionaries, and professionals of various kinds, some being sent to the colonies, such as America. (e) Finally, the ministers from Halle developed new seriousness about the Christian faith and practice.[168]

A second factor was at work in the Protestant church's evangelization of sub-Saharan Africa—the emergence of the Moravians. Around 1722, German-speaking Protestants from Monrovia sought refuge in Saxony. Count Zinzendorf allowed them to establish a village on his estate at

Herrnhut, with the hope that they would become a pietistic community within the Lutheran Church. By 1727, he had become the spiritual leader of the group, and their evangelical piety found expressions in Christ-centered mysticism, hymns, and liturgy.[169] They were a committed and zealous group of soldiers for Christ within the Lutheran Church. They reared and trained children within their community apart from parental supervision, as done at the Halle Orphan House. Life in their villages was like in a monastery. Due to increasing opposition from the "orthodox" Lutheran Church, the Moravians became a new church with a dedication to missions outmatched by no other Protestant group in the eighteenth century.[170] They sent missionaries to the West Indies in 1732 and Greenland in 1733; in 1735, Spangenberg led a party to Georgia in America. Other Moravian missionaries went to Ghana, Egypt, South Africa, and Labrador.[171]

A third factor was the Evangelical Revival, which touched both Europe and America, in which the missionary movement within the Protestant Church was rooted.[172] The so-called First Evangelical Awakening or Evangelical Revival began in Europe. In fact, according to Stephen Neil, a combination of this with the religious forces of "High Anglican piety, the mystical traditions, the pietism both of Halle and Herrnhut…led toward producing John Wesley and the Methodist movement in Britain."[173] This revival touched many countries in Europe: Germany, France, and Norway in the nineteenth century, and Geneva in the 1830s.[174]

The intellectual character of the period up to the eighteenth century was the age of enlightenment. Newtonian philosophy led to the exaltation of reason alone.[175] Deism was the main theological issue; people were to be content with a God who was remote and who seemed not to care, or who allowed things to be out of control. Vigorous opponents of deism included people like William Law, who wrote *A Serious Call to a Devout and Holy Life* in 1728 and had a profound influence on John Wesley; and Isaac Watts (1678–1748), a Congregationalist and the founder of modern English hymnology.[176]

Furthermore, during this same period, religious societies were common. The earliest was formed by "a group of young men in London about 1678, for prayer, reading the Scriptures, the cultivation of a religious life, frequent communion, aid to the poor, soldiers, sailors, and prisoners, and encouragement of preaching."[177] It is said that by 1700 there were nearly a hundred societies in London alone.[178] Many of the clergy of the time regarded those religious societies too "enthusiastic" and kept aloof. Samuel Wesley formed a religious society at Epworth in 1702.[179]

In this era, great personalities emerged as evangelists. Among them were George Whitefield (1714–70), who some consider the first and greatest evangelist of modern time. He was indeed a man "whose field of preaching stirred thousands both in England and in colonial America, when his astonishing eloquence vitalized the Great Awakening, about 1740."[180] Whitefield believed in predestination—that it was only the elect that would be saved. John Wesley (1703–91), a contemporary of Whitefield, preached "salvation was possible to all"[181] and not just for the elect. John Wesley was a great exponent of English evangelical pietism. Yet it was Whitefield who encouraged Wesley to take up open-air preaching. As a result, when Wesley died, England had 80,000 members in the Methodist Society, with about 1,300 local itinerant preachers, and in America 60,000 members and two hundred preachers.[182]

At a time when things once again seemed to die down spiritually in England, "the second Evangelical Awakening crossed the Atlantic from America to Britain in 1858."[183] In America at that time, the leading evangelists were Peter Cartwright (1785–1872), Charles Finney (1792–1875), Dwight L Moody (1837–99), and others. In Britain, they were William Booth (1829–1912) and Henry Drummond (1851–97).[184]

Formation of Missionary Societies

Following the spirit of revivalism in the churches of Europe, Britain, and America in the eighteenth century, most of the churches established missionary societies and boards.[185] The first missionary societies were the English Baptists, started in 1792; and the London Missionary Society (LMS), started in 1795 with the laudable aim of preaching the central gospel to the heathen without being tied to any particular form of church order or government. In actual fact, the LMS became before long the organ of the English Congregational body. Another was the Anglican Evangelical Church Missionary Society, started in 1799; and the British and Foreign Bible Society, which provided a notable example of interchurch cooperation, having a committee that was made up of half Anglicans and half Free Churchmen in 1804. America entered the list in 1810 with the American Board of Commissioners for Foreign Missions, mainly Congregational, and in 1814, with the American Baptist Missionary Board. Germany formed its first missionary society in 1824, the Berlin Society; Switzerland a little earlier in 1815 with the Basel Mission; Denmark in 1821, France 1822, Sweden 1835, and Norway 1842.[186] The Missionary Society of the Methodist Episcopal Church (now The United Methodist Church) formed in 1819.[187]

Some missionary societies not only sent people to Africa to engage in missionary work, but also to found their kind of churches. The Lutheran Church was probably the first Protestant missionary church to do that in Africa, as Heyling of Luebeck worked in Abbyssinia during 1634–36. In 1662, the Lutherans sent clergymen from Denmark to do missionary work in Ghana. The Moravians were in by 1726, often working through other churches, such as the Lutherans. Methodism came to Africa through the freed slaves. The ex-slaves came to Sierra Leone from England, Jamaica, and Nova Scotia in 1787–91; and to Liberia from America in 1822. The American Presbyterians date from 1833 in Liberia, Gabon, and Kongo. In 1867, Presbyterians entered Natal, and about 1874, the Scottish Presbyterians entered Malawi.[188] Many other churches followed later, and to this day, they are still coming to Africa.

Assumptions of Missionaries About Africa

As the European powers scrambled for African land, a process that the colonialists legalized by the Berlin Act (1885), the missionaries likewise engaged in comity agreements that almost amounted to missionary societies scrambling for African land also. Each missionary society ended up with a territory within which it was to develop its missionary work, leaving the people with no option to choose which brand of denominational church they would want. They had to accept the denomination that was assigned to its area.

The missionaries who came to Africa operated on a number of assumptions. They believed Africa was a "dark continent," a continent that had nothing to be proud of. They seemed to believe that Africa as a continent had no history, philosophy, culture, or religion of its own. At the turn of the twentieth century, John Taylor, a missionary of the Methodist Episcopal Church in what was then Southern Rhodesia, wrote:

> The people of these lands of Africa are primitive and hopeless...If there is a race of people in the world who are represented by the Lazarus in the story of the rich man, or "the one who has been robbed," in the story of the good Samaritan, it is the black man of Africa and his two hundred millions of brothers and sisters. Human helplessness is God's loudest language to those to whom He has given wealth and education and power. What a supply other peoples of the world have of life, of literature, of history, of at least something beautiful and true in their religious life of philosophy and genius. But all these are absent in Africa.[189]

A British Methodist missionary in West Africa wrote, concerning the allocation of missionaries:

> It is no reflection on the reduced number of men who now served in Africa that, in the main, those with an A.I life at Lloyds went to Africa and those with a first at Oxford or Cambridge to the east.[190]

The missionaries of that era never thought of an African as an equal. Some assumed an African does not think. Dom Toedosio Clemente de Gouveira, who in the 1940s became Archbishop of Maputo and later on was appointed Cardinal by the Pope, is quoted as saying, "The native is lazy, by nature and climate... And we must consider that the native is, in general, a child, although in a man's body. He thinks and reasons like a child...."[191]

On the contrary, we have the case of Muti Sikobele of Mozambique, a contemporary of John Taylor and possibly of Dom Toedosio Clemente de Gouveira, also. Sikobele was one of the earliest African pastors in the Methodist Episcopal Church, a gifted preacher and leader. Having been frustrated by the attitude of missionaries toward the Africans, Sikobele left his Methodist Episcopal Church circuit and formed his own church. In 1918, Sokobele wrote a letter to the Board Secretary Frank North in New York to lodge his complaint about missionaries. T. A. Beethem summarizes:

> He had "resigned to work with missionary Terril and Keys." He also attempted to explain why he had had to take this step. He accused Terril and Keys for not letting Africans work freely. "...They have not brothership with natives... When Bishop comes they will not let us have freedom to be or talk with him..."[192]

Considering his plan of action in Mozambique, Sikobele understood that there was no brotherhood between the white missionaries and the African preachers. He understood well what was going on. When the white missionary bishop visited their conference, the African partners were not allowed access to see and talk to the bishop. Furthermore, here was an African leader who had the courage to write to New York to the Secretary of the Missionary Society and openly and candidly tell him the reason he left the Methodist Episcopal Church to start his own. We are talking about an African leader of the church in 1918. For someone to say that an African thinks like a child might also mean the missionaries had a hard time understanding the African.

Likewise, the missionaries perceived of the African people as heathens who needed conversion and barbarians who needed western civilization. Hence, the early African preachers or evangelists or catechists were regarded as helpers. A closer look at the historical origin of many of the local churches in the rural areas shows that the African pastors preached and planted those churches. If those African pioneers in propagating the gospel penetrated the villages and towns of Africa to preach the gospel and to plant the churches among their own people, they were the ones who actually needed missionaries as helpers, and not the other way round.

There is a sense in which the missionaries and the colonialists were collaborators on some issues that concerned the African people. For example, the missionaries and the colonialists shared a common interest in eradicating anything that was viewed as African, either in perception or practice. African customs and traditions were considered barbaric and evil. Such practices had to be obliterated, supplanted with western customs or "civilized" Christian customs. In the main, while the colonialists talked of civilizing a barbaric humanity, the missionaries talked of converting the heathens who did not know the true and living God. Both the colonialists and the missionaries did not want to believe that the African people in sub-Saharan Africa had a past or their own ways of thinking. Harvey Sindima quotes Tom Colvin, a Scottish missionary, who wrote:

> Too often it was the Church that obliterated old society in the mistaken belief that a completely new form of society must be built in order to be Christian.[193]

Thus, evangelizing the Africans had to begin with making the new converts aliens in their own land—making African Christians deny their past, culture, and their way of thinking. They also had to admit that they did not know God. That kind of thinking is sometimes reflected in the kind of hymns that are still sung in our Sunday services.

Nevertheless, as the African church of today, we need to regard some of those things that happened as accidents of history. There is always today, when we can rise and move forward, and we can do so by learning from Paul who talked of the "freedom we have in Christ Jesus" (Gal. 2:4) or "the truth of the gospel" (Gal. 2:14), meaning the Gentiles did not have to become Jewish in order to be Christian. Now we know that we do not have to worship or sing like the Americans, British, Belgians, French, Germans, or Portuguese to prove that we are Christians. The time has come to promote music that is accompanied by drums, and any other musical instruments that the African Christians can lay their hands upon.

Various Denominations Evangelize the Continent

We can look at some of positive things that took place in the process of evangelizing and transforming Africa. In spite of all the negative things that we can say about the missionaries, the most important thing was that Africa received Jesus Christ, whom the continent did not know; and to this day, Christianity is thriving because of the preaching of him who was crucified and raised from the dead. Christ has become the symbol of hope and victory in the life of the African people. How was he communicated to the African people?

First, evangelism became central in the African church. The various churches from overseas nations came to Africa to proclaim Jesus Christ, baptize the converts, and plant local churches. As much as the African people claimed some knowledge about God, especially as the Creator, they had no knowledge of his Son, Jesus Christ. Thus, the thrust of the Christian message was to know God in Christ through the power of the Holy Spirit. For a long time, that evangelistic message of knowing God through Christ took central position in the Church's evangelical proclamation. To this day, if there is any topic that would bring many churches in Africa together, it is the ministry of evangelism. The gospel of Jesus Christ had to be shared or communicated by whatever means or methods were applicable in each situation. Disciples were made, and are still being made, through baptism and teaching or nurturing the converts.

In the effort to evangelize Africa, several methods have been used. One of the popular methods has been mass evangelism. Mass evangelism takes different forms according to tradition and theological background of a denomination. This has led churches to call mass evangelism by different names, such as mass evangelistic meeting, mass evangelistic mission, preaching mission, crusades campaign, marathon evangelism, and revival meeting. This approach to evangelism has been used practically by every denomination in Africa in its own way.

Second, the mainline churches realized the importance of education in evangelizing Africa. The emphasis on education stands out in the number of educational institutions each denomination established in Africa. Professor T. O. Ranger reminds us of the Roman Catholic slogan, "Who owns the schools will own Africa"; with the Protestants, it was, "Use the school to build the church."[194] Consequently, many of the great national leaders both in government and civil society in the last hundred years came through the hands of the church.

It is now common knowledge that the African Initiated Churches (AIC) first took the step to train African leaders at university level. They did so by joining hands with the Africans of the Diaspora, especially the African-American churches. It was the African-American institutions that first provided financial sponsorship for Africans to receive an education in African-American colleges and universities in the twentieth century. According to Harvey Sindima, examples of such beneficiaries are numerous and significant. The popularly known "Aggrey of Africa," James Emman Kwegyir Aggrey from Ghana, went to school at Livingstone College in North Carolina, USA, thanks to the bishop of the African Methodist Episcopal Zion in1902. Nmamdi Azikiwe, the first president of independent Nigeria studied at Tuskegee Institute in Alabama, USA. Ghana's first president, Kwame Nkrumah, who led his country to independence in 1957 thereby making it the first country to emerge from British colonial rule, studied at Lincoln University in Pennsylvania, USA. Earlier, A. B. Xuma and J. R. Rathebe of South Africa, as well as John Chilembwe and Daniel Malebu of Malawi, all in politics, were beneficiaries of scholarships arranged through African-American churches. The same was the case for Hastings Banda, who in the early 1960s became the first prime minister and president of Malawi.[195] From Zimbabwe, Obadiah Manjengwa received a scholarship to study at Livingstone College in the latter1940s. Upon completion and an unceremonious return home where he enrolled at Hartzell Theological College, he actually faced resistance. Only after a one to two year delay was he admitted to the conference for membership.

The challenge to train church leadership at university level created a new reality for the Methodist Church in Africa in the 1950s. The Liberia Conference had the connections to send its leaders for further education to America. But in the Central Africa Conference (including Angola, Congo, Portuguese East Africa, and Southern Rhodesia), Peter Shaumba was the first African clergy to earn a college degree, at Pain College in the United States. Onema Fama, the first Congolese national to serve as bishop in the Congo, graduated from Morningside College. Mathew Wakatama was the first Zimbabwean national to earn a masters degree—from the University of London. Likewise from Zimbabwe, Elish Mutasa, a medical doctor, graduated from the University of Edinburgh; Amon and Susana Dangarembwa earned MA degrees from the University of London; Davidson Sadza, a medical doctor, graduated from the University of London. Abel Tendekai Muzorewa, first Zimbabwean clergy to earn a college degree plus an MA from Scarritt College, became the first national to serve as bishop of Zimbabwe. Emilio de Carvalho, who studied in Brazil and then earned MA degrees in the United States from

Northwestern University and Garrett Theological Seminary, became the first national to serve as bishop in Angola. All of these leaders and many others who followed received their training in Britain, America, and Brazil, in the 1950s and 1960s. Similar opportunities were and are made available to other young African leaders by various church denominations in Africa to this day.

Third, evangelism happened through medical care. As with education, medical care, including healing from illness and alleviating pain, is God's will for every person. Many denominations established hospitals at some of their mission stations, and some of these hospitals became reputable medical centres because of the services they offered the surrounding communities. Some missionary medical doctors became household names because of their service in those mission hospitals. Some Christians may mistakenly view the establishment of church hospitals and clinics as simply a way to reach out and evangelize people. Rightly understood, however, health care is not merely a means to catch people for Christ but a way to care for all God's people as Christ did; it is a way to attend to the whole person and to alleviate pain caused by illness. Rightly or wrongly interpreted, medical care intrinsically has also been a way of evangelizing some people. To this day, some of the biggest and best functioning hospitals in African countries are the church hospitals established by the early missionaries.

Fourth, the gospel has reached many through the rise of African Initiative Churches. Originally called African Independent churches, the African Initiative churches came into existence around the 1920s. Their rise in existence became a challenge to the so-called mainline churches. Although some of these AIC were prompted and led by a few individuals who were either under disciplinary measures by some mainline churches or frustrated in one way or the other, generally speaking, they were motivated by the fact that the mainline churches had obliterated the African culture—that mainline churches had alienated African Christians from their culture and their people. Unfortunately, many missionaries during that time did not see that point; rather they interpreted the situation as influenced by *Ethiopianism*, as discussed earlier. These churches that broke away mostly from the missionary churches are scattered all over Africa—in West Africa, East Africa, Central Africa, and Southern Africa.

Fifth, evangelism has taken place through urban ministry. In the 1960s and early 1970s the African churches became conscious of the rapid growth of the African cities. That phenomenal growth resulted primarily from the political independence that many African nations attained. The cities attracted people from rural areas as cities became beacons of hope in for employment, education for children, and in improving one's life in general. The churches promoted ecumenical and denominational programmes that were known as *industrial mission of the church* (and other similar names)—to enable city churches to cope with the new urban challenges. There was tremendous response to this new ministry through the growth of the Christian communities in the African cities. All of a sudden the best pastors who used to find their way to a mission station appointment were being appointed to the big urban churches. Many of those pastors received training through workshops on urban ministries organized through denominational and inter-denominational efforts. Rapidly, ecclesiastical powers shifted from the mission centres to the urban churches.

Sixth, the gospel has been communicated through the rise of the Pentecostal and "mission-related" churches in Africa. Paul Gifford reports on a survey that was conducted by the Ghana Evangelism Committee of the entire country in 1986–87, and a repeat of the survey in 1993. A comparison of the two surveys was most revealing:

> The AIC [African Independent Churches] are in serious difficulty [in other words, on the decline]; the mainline churches are static if not decreasing [in other words, a good number were on the decline, just a few that were on the

> increase]; and substantial growth lies with new Pentecostal and "mission-related churches" [in other words, a massive percentage of growth of Christians lies here].[196]

Some of the reasons for such growth of Christians in the Pentecostal churches are: (a) They take the ministry of evangelism seriously. (b) In their worship they blend elements from Christian worship and contemporary worship. (c) They emphasize tithing. (d) They emphasize the ministry of deliverance. (e) They emphasize the message of success and prosperity.[197]

A good example of a mission-related church is the New Apostolic Church in Zambia. According to Gifford, "On 1 January 1982 it had 194,195 members; by 30 June 1994, 704,838; and by June 1996, 793,934, an increase of 409% in fourteen years."[198] The historical background of the church is that it originated in Britain in the nineteenth century, with structures that had twelve apostles. It came to Northern Rhodesia in 1928, then grew steadily until the 1980s when "it has increased enormously."[199]

The reasons for this rapid growth are several. The first, according to Gifford, "is professionalism. Buildings, furniture, vehicles, and equipment all testify to that. Its headquarters are far more impressive than the offices of the Christian Council or the Catholic Secretariat…in the mid-1990s all records were being put on computers…sermons laid down for evening and morning…Literature is prepared in five different languages of Zambia… A colour magazine, *Our Family*, is produced in South Africa and trucked to a wide circulation in Zambia. This is an impressively efficient operation."[200] The professionalism is also expressed through music, and the "music is linked to evangelization, which is pursued in imaginative ways."[201]

Other reasons include the fact that funds are provided from overseas. The church runs frequent seminars and workshops for its people, has a relief budget for its own members,[202] as well as handouts of food and clothes. There is no formal theological education for their pastors, but "there is enormous scope [of opportunity] to hold office, and a great chain of command along which aspirants are able to progress."[203] The church has connections with congregations overseas where they send their apostles for further training. There are several such churches or congregations situated in the major cities of Africa, and they have made an impact in the community and surrounding communities where they are situated. This is how Christians are being added to the body of Christ in many of these mission-related churches.

Summary

First, even though the colonialists and early missionaries to Africa assumed the absence of any type of civilization and lack of the knowledge of God among the African people, it is up to the church in Africa today to show that Africa has always known something about God, and that now they know God more clearly through Jesus Christ; and, indeed, to show that they have had their own type of civilization, partly characterized by the ancient "Sudanic states" in African history.

Second, the churches in Africa have continued with the basic methods of evangelization of Africa—evangelism, education, and medical care, as well as many other ways. Henry Venn, the secretary of the CMS from 1841 until his death in January 1873, expressed his missionary vision with a metaphor of scaffolding and building. There must be a great difference, he said, between the role of the mission and that of the church that emerged. He saw the mission's role as that of builders and scaffolding in a building. The scaffolding is used to build; then the builders remove it and go away. The missionary is not a resident pastor but an evangelist. Like scaffolding, he/she builds and then leaves. The church, then, is the building that remains, and that grows and flourishes according to its own gifts. He believed that the church in Africa should be an "African church," not a copy of the Church of England on African soil. He believed the Africans' special characteristics would mark their church African. He also saw the goal, the same goal that he worked towards as a missionary, as an African church that would be self-propagating, self-governing, and self-supporting. That goal needs to be realized still, and is being realized by some churches in Africa.

Third, there is much to learn from the growth of Christians in the Pentecostal churches. While mainline churches have a tendency to be critical of what is happening in Pentecostal churches, many of our churches practice similar methods. So it is important to be discerning about the features we embrace in our approach to evangelism.

(a) *Being born again*. Pentecostal churches take evangelism seriously, yet they often emphasize experiences of being born again and speaking in other tongues as the evidence of the Holy Spirit in the life of a Christian. Evangelism in The United Methodist Church also emphasizes the call to be born again as spiritual birth from above. Like most mainline groups, however, we call for spiritual rebirth not merely as an event but as part of the life-long process of Christian discipleship and growth toward Christian maturity.

(b) *Professionalism*. Ministry with professionalism and excellence is important and can glorify God. But evangelism is not a performance or a professionalized ministry; nor or is it located in certain offices of the church. Rather, evangelism belongs to all the people of God who know and love Christ.

(c) *Spirited worship*. Where Pentecostal churches blend elements of traditional and contemporary Christian worship, mainline churches in Africa have a lot to learn for the benefit of their congregations. There is no reason why mainline churches in Africa should pray and sing as if they were churches of Europe, Britain, or North America.

(d) *The discipline of tithing*. Pentecostal churches strongly emphasize the practice of giving through tithing. When I was serving as secretary to the Parliament of Zimbabwe in the 1980s, a Pentecostal pastor approached me in my office. Because tithing was their practice, he demanded to know salary figures of Parliament employees who were members his church. Naturally, I informed him that salaries were a confidential matter between the employer and the employee, and that I would not grant his request. But there has been a revival of the practice of tithing in some mainline churches in Africa. Some churches even declare that non-tithing church members will not be nominated to leadership positions in the church.

The practice of tithing needs reviving, and yet when tithing is practiced as a legal mandate or when it stands alone as the yardstick to evaluate the Christian worth of members, something may have gone drastically wrong. We need to remember that Paul's lesson from the spirit of giving he witnessed in the Macedonian churches was not about legalism but gratitude: "...they gave as much as they were able, and even beyond their ability" (2 Cor. 8:3).

(e) *Deliverance*. Pentecostal churches offer a ministry of deliverance from evil, a ministry for the whole church of Jesus Christ to embrace and to offer. Jesus delivered people from sin, death, and the devil, and sent his disciples to do likewise (Mark 3:15). Moreover, Jesus taught his followers to pray "deliver us from evil" (Matt. 6:13, KJV). Our churches need a theology and ministry of delivering people from the powers that destroy their life: demons, troubles and hardships, alcohol, disease, fear and innumerable dangers.

(f) *Success and prosperity*. The success and prosperity gospel is appealing to many in Africa today for obvious reasons. Poverty continues to reign and to menace innocent people in spite of the attainment of political independence from the 1960s by African countries. Nevertheless, African churches cannot afford to lose sight of the heart of Jesus' message: the kingdom of God. It was Jesus' message of God's kingdom (John 3:3) that inspired his followers' spiritual rebirth and commitment to love God wholly and serve humankind (Mark 12:29–31). In that message also was the promise, not necessarily of success and prosperity, but

> abundant life or life to the full (John 10:10). Thus, evangelism at its best seeks to introduce people to the gospel of Jesus Christ, "leading them to its acceptance, and guiding them in their growth toward its fulfillment in their lives."[204]

Ultimately, the challenge for mainline churches, African Initiated churches, and Pentecostal and mission-related churches in Africa is not so much the status of their church membership today. Rather, their challenge is how much of their missionary "scaffolding" has been removed from the African churches, and how much still remains. Or, how much of the church that remains standing, flourishing on African soil, resembles the image of Africa. These days in Africa are like the vision shared by John from the island of Patmos, when he talked about the heavenly city that no longer had a temple, for the Lord God Almighty and the lamb had become its temple. John went on to say:

> The city does not need the sun or the moon to shine on it,
> for the glory of God gives it light, and the Lamb is its lamp.
> The nations will walk by its light, and the kings of the earth
> will bring their splendor into it. (Rev. 21:22–24)

Chapter 7

The United Methodist Way of Evangelizing

Having reviewed the various approaches to evangelism of the African Church as a whole, beginning with and including the Christian communities in Egypt, Libya and North Africa, Ethiopia, the Kongo Kingdom, and the rest of sub-Saharan Africa church denominations, we now ask: What has been the role of The United Methodist Church (UMC) in this whole history of the evangelization of Africa? More specifically: What is the UMC approach to evangelism on the continent of Africa, and how has the UMC participated in evangelizing Africa?

The UMC in Africa has twenty-one annual conferences, four provisional conferences, and one missionary conference. These conferences are located in West Africa, West Central Africa, Southern Africa, and East Africa—organized under three UMC central conferences, namely, the Africa Central Conference (1920), the West Africa Central Conference (1980), and the Congo Central Conference (1988). This development reflects a phenomenal expansion of United Methodism in Africa with a history of 188 years in Liberia and a little less than 136 years in the rest of Africa. With respect for the vastness of the continent, annual conferences are established in various and different cultural and socio-political circumstances. In spite of the variation of contextual circumstances, however, there is still the UMC way of doing evangelism in Africa, which is rooted in a theological rationale and pragmatism that we share in common.

What is that underlying theological rationale and pragmatism that we share, that motivates and guides the UMC way of doing evangelism? To discover it, we must trace the history of the Methodist Revival Movement back to America, to Britain, and to the founder of the Methodist movement John Wesley himself. We do this not because we want to build copies of American Methodism or British Methodism, but because it is this historical and theological heritage that has coloured and influenced us as United Methodists in Africa. By exploring the genesis and evolution of the United Methodist way of evangelizing that has been given to us in Africa, we are more able to identify and understand the distinctive African UMC way of evangelizing Africa.

The Methodist Revival Movement in Britain

It was George Whitefield (1714–70), a clergyman of the Church of England, who originated the Methodist Revival. Just before Easter 1735, George Whitefield underwent an evangelical experience, which he afterwards described as a new birth.[205] After hearing that Wesley found peace of mind on 24 May 1738, Whitefield wrote to ask John Wesley to come and help him with work in Bristol where Whitefield was already preaching to great crowds. Wesley did not immediately accept Whitefield's invitation. Instead, he went to Zinzendorf's Moravian settlement at Herrnhut in Germany. On his return to England, Wesley spent time with a religious society of members of the Church of England in Fetter Lane in London—a religious society that was already familiar with Wesley's ideas, especially his new ones on the power of saving faith as the gateway to holiness. That society actually "marked a transition from the established religious society of the period to the new type of society which arose from Wesley's own experience and preaching."[206]

Again, Whitefield extended an urgent message of invitation to John Wesley to come to Bristol. Wesley had doubts about the whole affair, especially about involving himself in what he considered an unconventional approach to evangelism that included "field-preaching." Nevertheless, Wesley accepted the invitation. In the course of their preaching, both Whitefield and Wesley were surprised to find out that just as many people came to hear Wesley as had come to hear Whitefield. Rupert Davies reports that Wesley's "preaching was more striking,"[207] with reports of people crying out loud, roaring, and violently trembling all over.[208] Never had Wesley's converts, including in Bristol, ever gone through such an experience. As much as Wesley had originally thought the saving of souls outside of church buildings as almost a sin, the method of field-preaching that he learned from Whitefield became the principal means by which Wesley and his preachers proclaimed the gospel throughout England.[209]

Wesley's message for the revival movement was distinctive. Whitefield preached predestination—that God saved the few, called the elect to salvation through Jesus Christ, and predestined the majority of humankind to damnation. Therefore, the purpose of his evangelistic activity was to gather to Christ the elect who were predestined to salvation.[210] By contrast, John Wesley's message was that God wills all people to be saved, and that Christ died for all so that all may be saved.[211] In other words, Whitefield emphasized predestination, grace for the elect; Wesley emphasized "the grace of God for all" that is found in God's Son, Jesus Christ.

Philip Watson, a British Methodist theologian, summarized Wesley's message of God's grace as following:

(a) *All men need to be saved*. Why do they? Because all men are sinners. All men are either self-indulgent sinners like the Prodigal Son, or self-righteous sinners like his Elder Brother, or else, like most of us, they are something of both. Or as Paul says, "There is no difference, for all have sinned and fall short of the glory of God…" (Rom. 3:22–23)[212]

(b) "*All men can be saved*. How can they? Only one answer is possible: through Jesus Christ."[213] This is so because Christ died for all. This message struck home for many, to know that Christ died, not just for the elect, but all. "For God so loved the world that he gave his one and only Son, that whoever believes in him shall not perish but have eternal life" (John 3:16).

(c) *All men can know that they are saved.* Notice here that Wesley says, "can" know, not that they "must" know. He does not hold that a man cannot be saved unless he knows, as if knowing and being sure of it were a condition of salvation. What he contends is that everyone who is saved *can* have knowledge of it, and it is desirable that he should. We have no right to say that a person who is not sure is therefore not saved, but we do have the right to tell him he can be sure and to urge and help him to find assurance.[214]

(d) *All men can be saved to the uttermost.* The work of salvation is not completed with conversion, that is, with justification, adoption, the new birth or even with assurance. These things are only the beginning from which we must go on, Wesley insists, to "entire sanctification" or "Christian perfection." Sanctification means being made holy, and holiness is in Wesley's view, as we have seen, nothing else but love. It is love for God with all our heart and all our soul and all our mind and all our strength, in response to the love he has shown to us in Christ; and it is love for our neighbour "as ourselves" so that we treat our neighbour in the way God in Christ has treated us, showing to him the same Spirit of love.[215]

What was the organizational structure for the Methodist revival movement? John Wesley adopted a pragmatic structure that supported the movement's purpose. If there ever was a mission statement of the

Methodist Revival Movement, it might have been Wesley's answer to the question raised by eight Methodist leaders who met with him in London, June 1744:

> What may we reasonably believe to be God's design in raising up Preachers called Methodists? Not to form any new sect; but to reform the nation, particularly the Church; and to spread scriptural holiness over the land.[216]

Gradually, the Methodist Revival began to take root in Bristol, where John Wesley had originally been invited by Whitefield, then to London, Newcastle, and to the rest of England, Wales, Scotland, and Ireland. Bishop Kenneth Carder wrote that Wesley considered his evangelistic preaching as "the principal means by which converts are gathered into Christian fellowship and nurtured in faith and holy living."[217] Thus, Wesley adopted a pragmatic organizational structure for that nurture with these features:

(a) The *Methodist Societies*, the members of which were simply those that had "the desire to flee from the wrath to come" (Matt. 3:8; Luke 3:7). The Methodist societies served as arenas for proclaiming the gospel and for people to commit themselves as followers of Christ.

(b) *Class Meetings*, which originated as a way of gathering people to raise funds for the rebuilding of a Society New Room in Bristol, developed into a unit of Society membership (12 members). Classes became the small-group basis of Christian nurturance to new birth and saving faith, "the training ground of lay leaders, a potent instrument of evangelism."[218] The training of the laity for preaching, teaching, and leading in the propagation of the gospel was the genius of the Methodist Revival of the eighteenth century.

(c) *Bands* were smaller groups (3–5 members) "in which the higher reaches of Christian life could be explored,"[219] for "those who had experienced the new birth and were advancing towards Christian

> perfection."[220] After Wesley had been informed of some Methodists in the Kingswood night meetings spending time in prayer and praise and thanksgiving, he sought ways through bands to guide them for two reasons. He wanted to help them grow "in the grace and in the knowledge of our Lord Jesus Christ."[221] He also wanted to prevent them from the tendency of falling in "a narrowness of spirit, a party zeal, a being strained in our own bowels; that miserable bigotry which makes many so unready to believe that there is any work of God but among themselves."[222] Thus, there were men-bands, women-bands, married-people-bands, and single-people-bands.[223]

For Wesley and the People Called Methodists, evangelism involved preaching Christ in the Methodist societies, teaching and training converts through class meetings so that they would grow in the grace and knowledge of our Lord Jesus Christ through prayer and Bible study, and enrolling those who had experienced the new birth in bands for mutual support on the path towards Christian perfection.

What were the doctrines that underpinned the revival movement of the People Called Methodists? While the classical doctrines such as the trinity, the incarnation, atonement, and the church were presupposed in John Wesley's work and writings,[224] there are doctrines that Wesley often regarded as the fundamental doctrines of the People Called Methodists, that is, "those that worship God in spirit and truth."[225] John Wesley wrote: "Our main doctrines, which include all the rest are three—that of repentance, of faith and of holiness. The first of these we account as it were, the porch of religion; the next, the door; the third, religion itself."[226]

Wesley highlighted the following sub-headings under each of the three doctrines.

Repentance: God's image in man, the fall of man, the natural man, God's prevenient grace, which caused repentance.

Faith: the meaning of faith, justification, new birth or spiritual birth, and a sense of assurance.

Holiness or sanctification: perfection in the love of God, the goal of which was—for Wesley—summed up in Jesus' command to "love the Lord your God with all your heart and with all your soul and with all your mind and with all your strength… and your neighbor as yourself" (Mark 12:29–31). Such love, Wesley believed, led to both personal holiness and social holiness through practicing the works of piety and mercy. Since such holiness is a gift from the Holy Spirit, and holiness or sanctification is God's will for us, John Wesley contended that the doctrine of holiness does not necessarily encourage the danger of "enthusiasm," or charismatic religion.

Methodism in America and Evangelism

African United Methodism is a child of American Methodism. Our understanding of evangelism has always been shaped by our connection with The United Methodist Church in America. As such, there is need for African United Methodism to understand the historical factors that influenced American United Methodism. In addition to what American Methodism inherited from Britain, there are three attributes that were typical of American Methodism and that impacted evangelism in African United Methodism, namely: evangelizing the frontier, camp meetings, and the holiness movement.

Evangelizing the American frontier. In early American history, a cabin was a small house, built simply and crudely on private property, where the owner stayed apart from established and growing towns. Cabins also provided accommodation for the passersby, especially to those moving into the frontier. As America experienced waves of people migrating from the east to the west between 1810 and 1820, people often looked for such cabins as places of rest or simply to spend a night or two in safety from attackers.[227]

In the new frontier, Presbyterian pastors who went to frontier communities because of their high education were often drafted as school teachers. Most of the early Baptist preachers were farmers, having gone to America with the migration. The Methodist preachers, who were simply sent into the frontier by the bishops, had no attachment to a community institution or to a farm. They were free to open up new territory to sharing of the gospel.[228] Murray Leiffer, former Professor of Social Ethics and Sociology at Garrett Theological Seminary, described the itinerant Methodist preacher of the early nineteenth century as one motivated by two factors—"a distinct and divine call" and "a desire to lead men to a personal religious experience."[229] However, he goes on to say that the younger Methodist preachers gave more importance than old preachers to such motivations as "a belief that Christianity offers the solution to the social and political problems of a disorganized world."[230] Thus, it was such itinerant preachers who targeted the frontier cabins as a strategy of their evangelistic endeavours and were able to open new territory that developed into Methodist circuits. Those frontier itinerant preachers, who were also known as circuit riders, rarely had or enjoyed the privilege of parsonages; and it took them months to go round their circuits. Quite often, they would also be involved in camp meetings as they went round from place to place. That was part of evangelism in early Methodism in America.

Camp meetings. Lee and Sweet make their point at the outset that "the camp meeting was never an authorized Methodist institution."[231] However, Methodists in America were heavily involved in camp meetings. The history of American Methodism shows that the first camp meeting in America, which was held in Kentucky at the beginning of the nineteenth century, was an interdenominational meeting. Those camp meetings were associated with the Methodist Church because they were so much used by the Methodists themselves.[232] Some of the prominent leaders in the Methodist Church played a leading role in the history and development of camp meetings in America. Camp meetings seemed to be a natural and characteristic institution of the frontier, where the people felt the need to come together at least once every year. Since the Methodists were a leading church on the frontier, the camp meetings appeared to be a Methodist institution. Camp meetings created an appropriate climate for evangelism partly because of that social attraction and need for people to come together. Hence, early Methodist missionaries from the United States often testified in African churches that they had met Christ at camp meetings back home.

The Holiness Movement. John Wesley taught that Christians should love God perfectly. Again, Lee and Sweet say, "the doctrines of holiness and perfectionism, which had been emphasized in early American Methodism, were less and less emphasized in prosperous America after the Civil War [1865]."[233] Thomas Langford puts it differently, but without disagreement:

> After Wesley's time, stress upon perfect love for God as the culminating expression of Christian life continued in Methodist preaching. But there was fluctuation of emphasis upon, and divergence of interpretation of, Christian perfection. At times, reaching for conversion tended to eclipse the teaching of full Christian maturity. Theological interpretation of entire sanctification also varied.[234]

Langford goes on to say that in the 1830s there was an intensified search for personal holiness by some church members seeking the so-called "second blessing." By the 1850s, both clergy and laity in many denominations had been captured by the idea of holiness so much that by 1867 "the National Camp Meeting Association for the promotion of Holiness was established."[235]

As much as the holiness movement was interdenominational, "in its inception, it was essentially Methodist and distinctively American" (though later it moved across the Atlantic).[236] Its leadership continued to be Methodist, and with prominent personalities such as John S. Inskip and Phoebe Palmer. Phoebe Palmer was a doctor's wife from New York who became a strong leader in the movement.[237] "By the late 1800s a group called the *Come-outers* began to call for separation from non-Holiness churches; and through the last decades of the 1800s, a number of such groups established independent existence as denominations."[238] There were tensions within churches, including the Methodists, with each group claiming that they were more true to John Wesley's theological position with regard to sanctification. The principal issue that caused the tension involved the means and experience of sanctification. Some viewed sanctification as continuous Christian growth, while others viewed it as instantaneous or as involving two distinct experiences—conversion followed in time by baptism with the Holy Spirit, the sign of entire sanctification.[239]

Though Wesley used several terms to describe the new stage of life—perfection, holiness, entire sanctification, perfect love, and full salvation,[240] he defined "Christian perfection" as loving God with all your heart and with all your soul and with all your mind and with all your strength; and loving the neighbor as yourself (Mark 12:29–31). In answering the question Who is perfect, John Wesley pointed out that it was the one in whom is "the mind which was in Christ," and who "walketh as Christ walked," a man "that hath clean hands and pure heart," or that is "cleansed from all filthiness of flesh and spirit," or in whom is "no occasion of stumbling," and who, accordingly, "does not commit sin."[241]

John Wesley's theology was *Christo-centric* (Christ-centred). He did not use Pentecostal language of *second blessing* to define Christian perfection or sanctification. One of his favourite texts from Paul is, "I consider everything a loss compared to the surpassing greatness of knowing Christ Jesus my Lord… Forgetting what is behind and straining toward what is ahead, I press on toward the goal to win the prize for which God has called me heavenward in Christ Jesus" (Phil. 3:8, 13–14). Christian perfection for John Wesley was growing in grace in Christ Jesus through the power and guidance of the Holy Spirit.

It is important to know that "Methodist Episcopal Church interpreters on the whole stressed the growth in grace and tended to doubt the validity of two distinct events in Christian experience."[242] Consequently, wrote Langford:

> A statement adopted by the General Conference of the Methodist Episcopal Church, South, in 1894 affirmed the doctrine of the sanctification, but deplored the idea of two distinct events in salvation experience, the tendency to distinguish classes of Christians, and separatism. In 1896, the Methodist Episcopal Church (of the north) expressed a similar position.[243]

Many Holiness leaders felt they could not remain, and separation from both churches ensued.[244] Langford goes on to say that the growth of the movement was impressive, and has continued so in Protestant life, so much that "by 1971, more than one hundred fifty Holiness denominations and other groups were members of the Christian Holiness Association, successor to the National Camp Meeting Association."[245] The largest of these churches today are the Salvation Army, the Church of the Nazarene, the Wesleyan Church, and the Free Methodist Church. The personalities who played the leading roles in the Holiness movement in the mid-nineteenth century included Charles Finney, an American Congregationalist evangelist, and William Arthur, a British Methodist.[246] Some of the groups then included the Assemblies of God, the Churches of God, and the Pentecostal and Holiness churches, which had the largest membership.[247]

Realizing that Pentecostalism is growing so fast on the continent of Africa, we need to always keep in mind that Methodism's theological focus is *christocentric* (Christ-centered), while Pentecostalism is *pneumatocentric* (Holy-Spirit-centered). We must also remember that John Wesley associated the baptism of the Holy Spirit with conversion, and not with a second blessing.

Evangelization of Africa

The United Methodist Church first came to Africa by way of Liberia, as the African Methodist Episcopal Church. Former American slaves, who when freed returned to Liberia in 1822, introduced it. Among the first group of settlers that landed in Liberia in 1822 was Daniel Coker, a minister of the African Methodist Episcopal Church. Before landing back on motherland Africa, Daniel Coker organized those who were Methodists into a Society. Their landing on Liberian soil marked the introduction of American Methodism to Liberia and Africa.

Daniel was born of a white mother, Susan, and a slave father in Maryland; both parents worked for the same master. Daniel absorbed the rudiments of an education, then "in his youth ran away from his master to New York City."[248] In New York, Daniel Coker became a Methodist and was ordained a deacon by Asbury, having proved himself a powerful preacher. In 1801, Daniel moved to Baltimore, where Michael Coate, an elder in the Methodist Episcopal Church, helped him to purchase his freedom.[249] Daniel did not work full time as a preacher, but as a schoolteacher. It was in Baltimore, as he attended church, that he felt the pains of segregation in the life of the Methodist Episcopal Church. He worked hand in hand with Richard Allen (1760–1831), the leader of the Black movement in Philadelphia. Eventually, Daniel broke away to form the African Methodist Episcopal Church in 1816.

Daniel Coker's ambition was to return to Africa as a missionary, a dream that was fulfilled when he landed in Liberia with an organized Methodist Episcopal Society. African Central Conferences acknowledge and embrace the leadership role of Daniel Coker, who launched "one of the most formidable spiritual movements on the continent of Africa"[250] and consider him the father of Episcopal Methodism in Africa.

The spread of Episcopal Methodism from America to Africa, what is now The United Methodist Church in Africa, first took root in three areas: Liberia, the Congo, and Zimbabwe.

The Liberian Annual Conference. The first United Methodist Church

(Methodist Episcopal Church) missionary to Africa arrived in Liberia in 1833.[251] At the General Conference held in Philadelphia in May 1832, Bishops McKendree, Hedding, and Soule approved the first Methodist missionary to Africa, Melville Cox.[252] Cox was not well. Understanding his own situation, at the Wesleyan University Cox instructed his friend:

> "If I die in Africa you must come and write my epitaph."
> "I will," his friend replied, "but what will I write?"
> "Write," he replied, "let a thousand fall before Africa be given up."[253]

In February 1833, Cox arrived in Liberia. Thus, Africa was the first missionary field for The United Methodist Church, and Cox was the first missionary of the Methodist Society. Cox worked hard in organizing the Liberian Methodist Episcopal Church by holding a number of conferences that adopted the Articles of Religion and the General Rules according to "the moral discipline in general of the Methodist Episcopal Church in the United States of America."[254] On 21 July 1833, six months after his arrival in Liberia, Melville Cox died.

A medical missionary, Dr. Goshen, who arrived in Liberia in 1836, rendered significant Christian witness through his medical service. In 1858, Bishop Francis Burns, an African-American preacher from America, became the first missionary bishop for Africa until his death in 1863.[255] The Liberian Mission Conference became the Liberian Annual Conference in 1868.[256] It was administered from America, as it was part of the racially divided Black Central Conference system in the United States. The successor of Francis Burns was Bishop John Roberts (1866–75).[257] Neither Bishop Burns nor Bishop Roberts resided in Africa.

T*he Congo* M*ission* C*onference*. William Taylor was elected the first resident missionary bishop for Africa in 1884. He then became responsible for the supervision of the Liberia Mission Conference, as well as the Methodist work outside Liberia. United Methodist evangelistic and missionary work that existed outside Liberia in Africa was known as the Congo Mission

Conference of the Methodist Episcopal Church, and that work was credited to Bishop Taylor. Prior to his election to the episcopacy, Taylor had already become an evangelist of worldwide repute, who traveled on preaching campaigns and established self-supporting missions in South America, Australia, and India. He also traveled on evangelistic missions in the Cape Colony and Natal[258] in South Africa, although we do not have any report of him establishing missions in South Africa.

In the other countries mentioned above, Taylor, the evangelist, established those missions without the involvement of the Methodist General Mission Committee. He used the money that he received from the holiness movement camp meetings to send out missionaries. Because he believed in the idea of self-supporting missions, he expected the missionaries that were sent out to such missions to be self-supporting. Those missionaries rarely received any salary or other gifts. Consequently, many of them suffered or even died for lack of good medical care. In 1882, the General Mission Committee "denied the right of Taylor or any person other than its regular appointees to organize Northern Methodist churches outside the United States."[259] That action led to the closure of Taylor's missions in South America. Missionaries who had been sent there under his efforts were recalled. However, the General Mission Committee would not "dissolve the South India Conference, erected from Taylor's labors in 1880."[260]

A year after his 1885 election as the resident missionary, Bishop Taylor opened several mission stations in Angola and Congo. By 1890, he had opened another one in Inhambane, Mozambique. All of this Methodist Episcopal Church work in Africa, outside Liberia, became known as the Congo Mission Conference of the Methodist Episcopal Church. In May 1900 in Chicago, the General Conference of the Methodist Church took the following action in regard to the Congo Mission Conference:

> In the case of the Congo Mission Conference it shall be divided into two Mission Conferences as follows: (a) The

> East Central Africa Mission Conference shall include the work in East Africa south of the equator. (b) The West Central Africa Mission Conference shall include the work in West Africa south of the equator. (Disc., 1900, p. 260)[261]

Zimbabwe. Bishop Joseph Crane Hartzell, successor to Bishop Taylor in 1896, was responsible for introducing the Methodist Episcopal Church in southern Rhodesia when he secured a vast piece of land at Old Mutare—a former site for the town of Mutare in 1898. The mission work in Rhodesia in turn influenced the spread of the church in southern Congo through a missionary couple named Springer. Springer and his wife, former missionaries in Rhodesia, arrived at the copper mining camp of Kansanshi, on 18 July 1910. Herman Heinkel, another former missionary colleague in Rhodesia, joined the Springers.[262] They began work among the Lunda people of southern Congo at two mission stations, Musumba (Kapanga) and Kambove.

Two Africans, Jacob Maweni and Kayeka Mutembo, joined the missionaries. Kayeka Mutembo, a son of a former chief in southern Congo had been stolen as a boy by African slave traders from Angola. Having attended an American Board mission and converted to Christianity while in Angola, Mutembo prayed for a missionary to be sent to his people, the Lunda people. Therefore the advent of Springer and his wife as missionaries among the Lunda was an answer to prayer for Kayeka Mutembo. Bishop Lambuth and John Wesley Gilbert from the Methodist Episcopal Church, South, approached Chief Wembo-Nyama in Central Congo in February 1912.[263] Two years later on 12 February 1914 they opened the Wembo-Nyama Mission.[264]

Bishop Hartzell was also responsible for implementing the 1900 Chicago General Conference resolution to create two mission conferences from the Congo Mission Conference. The East Central Africa Mission Conference, which included work in Mozambique and in Zimbabwe, was created at St. Andrews, Mutare, at its first session, in 1901.

Throughout the years, Methodism flourished not only within the areas mentioned above, but also to neighbouring countries such as Malawi, Zambia, and South Africa. Methodism has moved to East Africa, where we now have the East Africa Annual Conference, which embraces Burundi, Kenya, Rwanda, Sudan, Tanzania, and Uganda. In West Africa, Methodism is no longer confined to Liberia. Through the creation of the U*nited* Methodist Church by the merging of the Methodist Church and the United Evangelical Brethren Church in 1968, we now have the Nigeria Annual Conference and the Sierra Leone Annual Conference—all part of The United Methodist Church. United Methodism has since moved to other West African countries as well, such as Ivory Coast, Cameroon, and others.

This marvelous work of evangelism by United Methodists on the continent led to the organization of the three Central Conferences—the Africa Central Conference founded in 1920, the West Africa Central Conference founded in 1980, and the Congo Central Conference founded in 1988. These three central conferences together embrace twenty-one annual conferences, one provisional conference, and one missionary conference at the time of this writing.

African United Methodist Way of Evangelizing

The question before us is What are the approaches to evangelism that are being used by The United Methodist Church in Africa to transform Africa so that increasingly Africa becomes a Christian continent? After all, there is evidence all around us that in this twenty-first century Africa is becoming the home to one of the largest Christian communities in the world. That being the case, what approaches to evangelism are African United Methodist churches using to make a holistic witness, build the church, and grow the Christian presence on the continent?

Prior to naming those points of commonality, let us recall the amazing diversity within which we observe and explore these common approaches to evangelism.

We have already pointed out that due to the vastness of Africa as a continent, a variety of geographical, cultural, and contextual factors impact the three regional United Methodist central conferences. Clearly, there can be no one way to approach the ministry of evangelism in all of these situations.

In earlier chapters, we brought forward the diverse historical influences from the Methodist Revival in Britain and the American heritage of the camp meetings and the holiness movement. We can see how all those factors have influenced The United Methodist Church in Africa and the way we do evangelism in Africa.

Moreover, there are the diverse international influences. The historical base of African United Methodism is clearly from America, even mistakenly identified at times as the American Methodist Church! And yet, United Methodist missionaries came to Africa from a number of countries, including Britain, Germany, and Scandinavia.

With this variety of sending groups came theological diversity as well. Annual conferences in Africa have received missionaries who hold divergent views on key issues such as sanctification. As we saw earlier, some held the official church position, affirming growth in Christian love while deploring the idea of two distinct events in salvation experience. Others, influenced by the holiness movement, emphasized the importance of a conversion plus a second blessing in which one receives the Holy Spirit. Thank God, John Wesley modeled tolerance toward a few of his close associates who talked of a second blessing! Wesley's position never changed; he associated the receiving of the Holy Spirit with continuous conversion, not as a second blessing.

Generally speaking, the diversity may not have adversely affected ordinary church members in Africa, and many pastors as well, who were less aware of different theological orientations at work. And yet, theological diversity could be observed not only from one missionary to another, but also from one annual conference to another, depending upon which missionary group was more influential in pioneering those African annual conferences.

The rich and sometimes troublesome diversity described here—cultural, historical, and theological—is what has been inherited by the African annual conferences. It has impacted our understanding and practice of evangelism. And yet, because the African annual conferences share a common historical and theological heritage, we can see and lift up important points of commonality that characterize the United Methodist way of doing evangelism in Africa.

Sunday preaching. Evangelism in United Methodism in Africa is anchored in Sunday preaching. The history of African United Methodism teaches us that Sunday worship presents a great opportunity for evangelistic preaching. An African United Methodist preacher, whether an ordained clergyperson or a lay preacher, is aware of the opportunity for the proclamation of the gospel that comes with the regular Sunday worship service. He/she is aware of the fact that every congregation is like the field that Jesus describes in the kingdom parable of the wheat and the weeds—every congregation consists of both and they are always growing together (Matt. 13:24-30). African preachers know as Wesley did that every congregation includes persons who are "self-indulgent sinners like the Prodigal Son, or self-righteous sinners like the Elder Brother, or else like most of us they are something of both."[265] This understanding of human nature and of the church motivates the preacher to approach the pulpit with the task of persuading men and women to commit their lives to Christ and to continue their spiritual upbringing in him. For some pastors, the congregation has proved to be the most fertile ground for evangelistic preaching that leads people to abundant life—where people begin to realize their potential in life, and end up serving God and society in one way or the other.

Effective evangelistic preaching often lifts the great promises of the gospel, such as:

> "Ask and it will be given to you; seek and you will find; knock and the door will be opened to you" (Matt. 7:7).
> "Come to me, all you who are weary and burdened, and I will give you rest..." (Matt. 11:28).
> "Here I am! I stand at the door and knock. If anyone hears my voice and opens the door, I will come in and eat with him, and he with me" (Rev. 3:20).

Several African preachers are finding joy in taking up the task of proclaiming such biblical promises that lift Christ Sunday after Sunday, while at the same time hurting people find healing as they respond to the gospel of Jesus Christ.

Allow me to share my personal viewpoint. I envy a pastor who is in the same pulpit Sunday after Sunday, preaching and expounding the biblical promises of God to his/her congregation. As much as such preaching may require hard work through planning, it is at the same time rewarding to both the congregation and the preacher. I have always believed being such a pastor is the best appointment that an ordained United Methodist clergyperson can have.

For example, when I was on leave from my post at Africa University during June and July 2010, I decided to work in my garden more than I have ever done before. As long as I was at home for those sixty-one days, there was not a single day I did not go in the garden, sometimes twice or thrice in a day. I sowed the seeds and transplanted the seedlings. I saw to it that the seedlings were watered, that the beds were mulched. Time and again, I found myself attending to each vegetable plant individually, killing the worms that I found near the plants, applying all kinds of pesticides so that the plants would grow properly, and so we would have vegetables for the family. I could not help thinking of the fact that a pastor-evangelist is like a gardener—one who knows his/her congregation and community; who moves around among the people and listens to their problems, their fears, and aspirations; who goes where the parishioners live and sits among them (see Ezk. 3:15) in order to understand them. It is an approach such as this that leads pastors to be great preachers and pastor-evangelists in their congregations. Such pastor-evangelists have emerged again and again in the African annual conferences. Such pastors do not depend on wandering evangelists (conference or district evangelists) because they can do the job.

Focus on making disciples. African United Methodism teaches us an evangelism that introduces people to Christ, and then nurtures the converts through caring and teaching into an understanding of the new faith to which they are called. Accepting Jesus Christ must not be confined to an initial verbal commitment; faith in Christ means "continuing growth of persons as members of the believing, redeeming, worshipping-learning community which is the church."[266] Members need to both believe and serve Christ so that they continue growing toward the fulfillment of the faith in Christ-like living. That seems to be what Jesus had in mind when he commissioned his eleven disciples in Galilee, "Therefore, go and make disciples of all nations, baptizing them in the name of the Father and of the Son and of the Holy Spirit and teaching them to obey everything I have commanded you" (Matt. 28:19–20). Obviously the key words concerning making disciples in this text are *baptizing* and *teaching*. Baptism assumes that the gospel has been heard or communicated and the individual now believes in the gospel (Rom. 10:14). The next stage is that they receive teaching to fully appreciate the meaning of the gospel, the transformation it brings, and the way of life it entails.

When The United Methodist Church was introduced to Africa, one of the challenges that the church faced was illiteracy. Illiterate persons were converted to Christianity, but how could they possibly grow and become mature Christians without the ability to read the Bible and other Christian literature? The first book that many African Christians learned to read was the Bible. Some of the early African Christians lived a Christian life in which they read no other book at home other than the

Bible. My own mother, who was converted to Christianity as a young girl and died in 1999 at the age of 105 years old, was such a person. When old age prohibited her from going to work in the field, reading the Bible became a daily delight (see Ps. 1:2).

Fighting against illiteracy in the early years of Methodism was one of the reasons the mission stations were established all over the continent, and such mission stations became the best arena for making disciples. Our mission stations today continue to be the best arena for evangelization. At our mission stations, thousands of young people spend their prime formative years in a Christian environment. What an opportunity for the church to decisively and persuasively impact the lives of young people, so that they will in turn make an impact on the future of Africa!

The challenge at our mission stations may no longer be illiteracy. Rather, our pastors and teachers are focusing on Christian discipleship, making sure young people know that they are being called to Christ to serve, and that accepting Christ and aspiring to earn the highest grades in the classroom are indeed what Christian discipleship is about. Arias and Johnson write, "Disciples are not born, they are made, and it takes a whole lifetime without a graduation in sight!"[267] The United Methodist Church in Africa—in the mission stations, in the rural areas, and especially in the urban areas—is currently applying the Matthean method of making disciples, transforming Africa through evangelism and Christian education.

Revival meetings. The church in Africa believes in revival meetings as a way of doing evangelism. The churches are propelled by a series of revivals. In Zimbabwe, every circuit is expected to hold four revival meetings in a year. In addition, revival meetings take place at the district level and beyond the district level. A number of African conferences have preserved memorable historical records concerning the practice of revival meetings in their histories.

Alf Helgesson, a former missionary in Mozambique, shares experiences from the beginnings of Protestantism in the Maputo Region when Methodist Episcopal Church and other Protestant groups were small in number. For that reason, they worked closely with one another and worked closely with the Roman Catholic Church, which was close with the Portuguese government. So what happened within the community of one Protestant church affected all the others. Helgesson writes:

> We recall that, even before the first arrival of the Wilcox couple [possibly one of the missionaries] at Inhambane, some beginnings of Protestant missionary work had taken form at the Delagoa Bay, where Lourenco Marques was by then growing into importance. Yosefa Mhalamhala, who was the forerunner of the Swiss Presbyterian Mission in that region, had settled at Ricatla, 30 kilomitres north of Lourenco Marques, preaching enthusiastically in spite of official Portuguese suspicion. In 1885, a great spiritual awakening erupted. Two more years passed before the first Swiss missionaries settled in the Lourenco Marques region. They were Rev. Paul Berthoud and his wife, who arrived at Ricatla, together with three Tsonga evangelists from the Transvaal and their families on July 9, 1887. The revival had by then spread all over the region, and the missionaries could step into the ongoing, lively movement, which also affected enterprising Tsonga in Lourenco Marques. One of these was Jim Ximungana. He had become rich by selling liquor but was now an evangelist, preaching the gospel and witnessing of his radical conversion.[268]

There are also examples of unrecorded revivals that took place in several of the annual conferences but went unnoticed especially if they were championed by the African preachers. Alf Helgesson writes about Tizora Navess's revival preaching, which he learned about from the latter's son. Tizora Navess was one of the pioneer African pastor-teachers in Mozambique.

> His son, Rev. Nataniel Navess remembered his father being away from home for several months in 1916–1917, even reaching the Transvaal. When he came home, he had tales to tell of huge crowds gathering to hear pastor Tizora preach "about Moses and God who liberated the people of Israel." Evidently, a *revival*, possibly with political overtones, was in the air.[269]

In spite of that, Tizora Navess was not ordained. Yet, "at the Annual Conference of 1917, larger numbers, both children and adults, than ever before were reported having been baptized since the previous Annual Conference."[270]

One cannot talk about the Methodist Church evangelizing Zimbabwe without mentioning the 1918 Revival. That revival in Zimbabwe started at Old Mutare mission in June 1918, seventeen years after the organization of the East Africa Mission Conference in 1901. Some of us are lucky in that we were able to see, talk to, and even interview some of the eyewitnesses of that revival. The impression one gets from the interviews and especially the reports that are recorded in the *1919 Rhodesia Mission Conference Minutes* is that the Holy Spirit revived the seventeen-year-old Missionary Conference in a mighty way.

For example the following are some words by eyewitnesses of the 1918 Revival in Zimbabwe:

(a) The Committee on Resolutions reported an acknowledgement of the revival as follows:

> Since God has so graciously answered the prayers that have ascended to Him for Africa from the missionaries, the native Christians and the church at home, our hearts are filled with gratitude to him for the revival that visited our

work beginning last June, and which reached almost every heart.[271]

(b) The District Superintendents reported:

> Just as it should be, the past year has been unquestionably our best year. Great new spiritual values have been realized. Every centre has been shaken with a fresh spiritual blast until heathen people have seen a great light and felt the presence of a new power.[272]

(c) Another report about the impact of the revival came from the Committee on the State of the Church, which stated:

> Last June there came upon our native teachers a baptism—a Pentecost. We are not impressed with gymnastics that some went through, but a large number of our men became flaming fires with a heavy burden for their people rolled upon them.[273]

The revival of 1918 made an impact on the annual conference. It touched both African pastor-teachers and missionaries; it was experienced conference-wide; there were a high number of converts, and a good number of young men responded to God's call to the ordained ministry. It affected the giving habits of people in terms of church offering, and made people and even the church realize their potential.

Another revival took place in Central Congo. In February 1912, Bishop Lambuth and John Wesley Gilbert reached Chief Wembo-Nyama in Central Congo and were received with enthusiasm.[274] The bishop opened the Wembo-Nyama Mission on 12 February 1914. The emphasis of the mission was fourfold: (a) industrial, (b) education, (c) medical, and (d) evangelism.[275] In December 1931, the missionaries invited Gilbert Ridout from Kentucky to conduct a revival at Wembo-Nyama Mission. The revival drew many people from near and far. A multitude of clergy and laity alike received the power and baptism of the Holy Spirit.[276] One of the memorable results was that by 1935 the number of *Atetera* (an ethnic group) preachers increased from forty-two to 165, and church membership increased from 635 to 5,026.[277] It is not surprising that revivalism and mass evangelistic meetings have become a common pattern and practice of evangelism by United Methodism in the Democratic Republic of Congo.

Such historic revivals have taken place in almost every annual conference of the United Methodists in Africa, resulting in annual conferences' regarding revival meetings as an important way of doing evangelism. Samuel Dzobo, an elder in the Zimbabwe East Annual Conference, wrote a Master of Theological Studies dissertation in evangelism while at African University in which he comments on the way United Methodists in Mutare view their relationship to revivals.

> Revivals are main events on a United Methodist congregation's calendar. Each local church or charge will have a minimum of four revival meetings as organized by the youth, women, men and the evangelism committee for the local church. The district will also have a minimum of four revival meetings. The conference usually has three revival meetings, but the women's revival meetings or the conventions dominate because of the large numbers of people who attend.[278]

He goes on to say:

> The revival meetings' success has contributed to why both clergy and laity leadership would define evangelism in connection with revivalism. Revivalism in Mutare is connected to the history of the 1918 revival because out of the 1918 revival, the church grew with Africans preaching the gospel to their own villages and communities. [279]

All annual conferences of The United Methodist Church in Africa tend to use the terms *revival* and *evangelism* interchangeably because of the significant role revival meetings play. The gospel reaches both backsliders and unbelievers through revivals conducted at all levels—local church, district, and conference.

Class meetings. Evangelism in The United Methodist Church in Africa uses *class meetings* to connect evangelism with Christian education. Here, evangelism and Christian education work hand in hand. We have already noted that with the Methodist Revival Movement in Britain, *class meetings* developed into a unit of society membership (12-member classes), "the training ground of lay leaders, a potent instrument of evangelism."[280] In class meetings, the first and second generations of Methodists in Africa were introduced to catechism. Apart from the Bible, the catechism booklet was the only literature used in the class meetings. Although it had its limitations, the catechism was effective; Christian parents even bought copies so that they could teach their children at home. Still today class meetings are the main means by which United Methodist churches across Africa meet church members' need to grow in their understanding of the Christian faith, the Bible, and what is essential and not essential in the Christian walk. Class meetings serve as the training ground, not only for membership in church, but also for mission in the community and society at large.

In Angola, for example, the class meetings have played a significant role as a vehicle for evangelism. The United Methodist class meetings are held during the week in small buildings in local areas closest to members of the church. On Sundays, they all meet centrally at the church building. Because of the evangelistic nature of these class meetings, classes sometimes grow into congregations.

In Zimbabwe, a variation on the class meeting arose called *sections*, which took the place of class meetings. This new phenomenon began in the 1970s. The Reverends Zebediah Marewangepo, then pastor of St. Mark United Methodist Church of Highfield, Harare, and Isaac Mapipi

Mawokomatanda, then pastor of St. Timothy United Methodist Church of Mabvuku, Harare, were instrumental in that transition. Sections are like classes but are organized geographically according to members' residential locations. The number of members in a section usually ranges from ten to twenty, depending on the concentration of members in a particular geographical area. In big congregations, the number of people in a section could be as many as thirty, or more. The main thrust of section meetings is evangelism and teaching. Section members meet in homes of members during the week for prayers and teaching. Or they may meet in homes of neighbours who invite them in to hold such prayer meetings. As a result, many people become members of the church through the evangelistic ministry of the section meetings. It is also through the section meetings, as in class meetings, that Christians become aware of their potential as disciples and the gifts God has given them to serve both in their churches and in the community.

Refugee camps. Evangelism in East Africa flourished through *refugee camps* in the 1990s where evangelism took the form of relief work. Writing about the expansion of The United Methodist Church in East Africa, Jean Ntahoturi, an elder in the East Africa Annual Conference who studied for the MTS degree in Evangelism at Africa University, Faculty of Theology, wrote a dissertation under my supervision in which he assesses how evangelism took place in conflicted areas where large portions of the population had become refugees. Ntahoturi likens the results of the conflict in the Great Lakes region, especially following the Rwandan genocide of 1994, to the persecution that followed the stoning of Stephen in Jerusalem, causing Christians to flee from Jerusalem.[281] Similarly, Ntahoturi says, the whole Great Lakes region was destabilized; people fled to neighbouring countries for refuge, such as East Congo, Kenya, Uganda, and Tanzania. This destabilization traces back to 1972,[282] which is an indication of how long many people of the region lived in refugee camps. That means children born in refugee camps might have lived there for two decades or more without knowing their homelands.

Destabilization in the region of the Great Lakes created not only human crisis, but opportunity for The United Methodist Church (as well as other church groups) to spread the grace of Christ through relief work and relationships among refugees. United Methodist outreach extended from Burundi and Rwanda to other neighbouring countries. Ntahoturi points out the way the church spread: Ferdinand David Egessa made contact with Rev. Solomon Muwanga, a Ugandan who had helped found The United Methodist Church in Uganda, to help them establish the same in the western province of Kenya in 1993.

In Tabora, Tanzania, as refugees began to arrive in 1972, and in Kigoma and Kagera in 1994, The United Methodist Church began to make its witness within the refugee camps. The church also made its witness felt among the Rwandan refugees who fled to the eastern Congo. In 2001, in another refugee camp called Mtabila, a United Methodist church was established with a membership of 8,500. That situation enabled The United Methodist Church to grow to the strength of 15,000 members.[283] Ntahoturi, who during one long vacation from African University worked in some of the refugee camps, reported one conversation with a number of converts to The United Methodist Church who spoke of their commitment to Christ and their discovery of the Bible. They reported how studying the Bible strengthened them, gave them a positive outlook on life, and strengthened their families, which in some cases had been completely shattered and had family members that were missing.

By the end of the 1990s, United Methodist evangelistic work extended into Burundi, Kenya, Rwanda, Sudan, and Uganda—all coordinated by the Burundi Annual Conference, which in 1998 changed its name to East Africa Annual Conference, with fifteen districts.[284] One cannot help but think about all of the people in refugee camps throughout Africa who are not just numbers but individuals suffering. The church is among them as salt and light, and continues witnessing to E*manuel*, God [is] with us.

Mass evangelism. United Methodists have used several mass evangelism methods in Africa, which in addition to camp meetings include conventions, crusades, open-air crusades, marathons, music galas, and preaching missions. The degree to which the annual conferences have used these various methods of evangelism depends on their situations.

Social principles. The United Methodist Church in Africa bears witness to Christ through commitment to its Social Principles. Right from the outset, The United Methodist Church in Africa taught that the gospel is both personal and social. This way of understanding the gospel traces back to Methodism in the United States and in Britain, and to John Wesley himself who in the eighteenth century wrote, "First, Christianity is essentially a social religion; and that to turn it into a solitary one, is to destroy it."[285] This holistic understanding of the gospel led John Wesley and the early Methodists to minister vigorously to the poor, prisoners, slaves, the children of the poor who needed education, and other persons affected by social problems.

The Rhodesia Annual Conference in the 1960s and 70s (in what is now the Zimbabwe Episcopal Area), organized Christian Social Concerns Committees in every church circuit in order to find Christian solutions to social problems aggravated by racial political tension. The committees spread the message of Christian social action, urging individual Christians and the church at all levels to be involved in the political arena of life. While the committees encouraged members to associate with the political party or movement of their choice, they advised churches to avoid endorsing any political party. Rather, the churches were to endorse the Christian social principles, which uplift humankind and promote the common welfare of all the people, while at the same time condemn political practices that undermined the dignity of humankind.[286]

So attractive was the boldness with which The United Methodist Church would speak the truth concerning the political situation that whenever the Rhodesia Annual Conference held session, the public paid attention. People waited to hear a message of hope, which newspapers or *Umbow*, the conference paper, usually released. This was a United Methodist way of proclaiming the gospel. As a result, many people associated with The United Methodist Church. The same has happened in other countries as well, where political conditions called for the witness of The United Methodist Church in those places.

United Methodism is thriving on the continent of Africa. Today it is proud of its twenty-one annual conferences, four provisional conferences, and one missionary conference. Earlier on, we talked about Christian discipleship being central to the African United Methodist thrust on the continent, its two arms being evangelism and education. In 1988, the General Conference of The United Methodist Church approved the establishment of Africa University—a university for all of Africa, which opened its doors to the first students in March 1992. Its mission statement reads:

> Education is the fundamental means of fulfilling individual needs and personal development, achieving the goals of society, and advancing culture and economy. The mission of Africa University is to provide higher education of high quality, to nurture students in Christian values, and to help the nations of Africa achieve their educational and professional goals. Africa University will play a critical role in educating the new leadership of African nations.

Although Africa University began with two faculties, today it has six faculties and one institute: Agriculture and Natural Resources, Education, Health Sciences, Humanities and Social Sciences, Management and Administration, Theology, and an Institute of Peace, Leadership, and Governance. The establishment of Africa University was a grand step by The United Methodist Church in the evangelization of Africa.

Summary

These summary comments highlight three important factors regarding evangelism in The United Methodist Church in Africa.

First, evangelism is central to the UMC and its mission in Africa.

The annual conferences with their districts and circuits and/or local churches have always made efforts to create an evangelistic spirit within the membership. Under the leadership of the pastors, the churches assist in planning and promoting special evangelistic preaching services on all occasions, convenient or inconvenient, in season and out of season (see 2 Tim. 4:2). As part of creating this evangelistic spirit and awareness, some local churches visit in homes to offer Christ. They offer friendly visitation by which to lead the inactive members back into the redemptive community, and to minister to the elderly and shut-in. They map new frontiers for the purpose of reaching out to new people for Christ's sake.

Second, revival meetings are one of the most favoured methods of doing evangelism in Africa by annual conferences of The United Methodist Church. Whether or not United Methodists in Africa are simply attached to revival meetings due to inheritance from a revival movement, the revival meetings are an effective means of grace by which many people make commitments to Christ. Bringing together large numbers of Christians in the name of Christ proves to be a powerful way of witnessing for Christ. United Methodists in great numbers leave their homes, travel a day or two to these great meetings where people may number five thousand and where they may stay for three to five days. Members of the church find spiritual strength; many new converts find faith.

Third, at the beginning of the twenty-first century, annual conferences of The United Methodist Church in Africa adopted the Matthean concept of disciple-making as the theme for their evangelism. This theme is based on the text, "Therefore go and make disciples of all nations, baptizing them in the name of the Father and of the Son and of the Holy Spirit, and teaching them to obey everything I have commanded you. And surely I am with you always, to the very end of the age" (Matt. 28:19–20).

According to Matthew, the disciple-making mode of evangelism is a mandate to every congregation to go to every community and every nation to make disciples. The mandate is not to disciple some of the people but *all* (Matt. 28:19), baptizing them in the name of the Father, of the Son, and of the Holy Spirit, and teaching them the Christian faith. No evangelist is in a better position to achieve the Matthean disciple-making method of evangelism than the pastor. He or she can evangelize the community, and can guide the Christian education programmes for the various age groups of the congregation, so that everyone grows toward Christian maturity and the realization of their potential. Hence, Arias and Johnson's saying: "Disciples are not born, they are made, and it takes a whole lifetime, with no graduation in sight…Evangelism without discipleship is not evangelism in the New Testament sense, according to the Great Commission."[287]

Interestingly, two BD Hon. graduates from the Faculty of Theology at Africa University in 2009 presented papers, researched separately and in two different United Methodist communities. They came up with very similar findings with regards to evangelism. Joe Samalenge, from the Democratic Republic of Congo, wrote on "The Relevance of the Methods of Evangelism used in The United Methodist Church in the Mutare District [in Zimbabwe]: A Case Study of Hilltop Circuit," for which he conducted interviews. In answer to the research question "How did you become a member of Hilltop United Methodist Church?", the highest percentage of respondents (29.33 percent) were born and raised in The United Methodist Church at Hilltop. The lowest percentages named circuit revivals and crusades.[288] Similarly, Paul Mazumba from Zimbabwe, in "A Critique of the Methods of Evangelism Used by The United Methodist Church in Harare: A Case Study of the Harare Central District," asked laity of Harare Central District to indicate any of three ways through which they became members. Mazumba reported that about 75 percent, the highest percentage, indicated that they were brought up in a Methodist family.[289]

The findings of the two papers show us that the disciple-making method of evangelism proves to be one of the best approaches to evangelism. The United Methodist Church needs to continue emphasizing the link between evangelistic outreach and Christian education; the two go hand in hand in our local churches. The goal of evangelism is not people merely making commitments to Christ; it is people becoming true disciples; it is converts learning more about the whole Christian faith, especially Christ himself in the context of the Christian community. This is the Christ who said, "I came so that they may have life, and have it to the full" (John 10:10).

Endnotes

1 David B. Barrett, "AD 2000: 350 Million Christians in Africa," *The International Review of Missions*, Vol. LIX, No. 233 (January 1970), 47.
2 *Christianity Today* (13 July 1998), 22.
3 *The General Secretary's Report to the Eighth Assembly of the World Council of Churches*, Harare, Zimbabwe, 3–4 December 1998.
4 *The Interpreter's Dictionary of the Bible* A-D, 79.
5 Henry Chadwick, *The Early Church* (New York: Penguin Books, 1971), 64.
6 Eusebius, *The History of the Church from Christ to Constantine*, Book 2:16 (New York: Penguin Books, 1983), 89.
7 G. S. P. Freeman-Grenville, *The New Atlas of African History* (New York: Simon & Schuster, 1991), 52.
8 Ibid., 133.
9 John Ernest Leonard Oulton and Henry Chadwick, *Alexandrian Christianity* (Philadelphia: The Westminster Press, 1954), 16.
10 Correct or conforming to the usual beliefs
11 Chadwick, *The Early Church*, 64.
12 Tony Lane, *The Lion Concise Book of Christian Thought* (Sydney: A Lion Book, 1984), 20.
13 *The Interpreter's Dictionary of the Bible*, Vol. E–J (Nashville: Abingdon Press, 1962), 181.
14 Eusebius, *The History of the Church from Christ to Constantine*, 148.
15 Ibid., 213.
16 Ibid.
17 W. H. C. Frend, *The Early Church* (Philadelphia: J. B. Lippincott, 1966), 94.
18 Eusebius, *History of the Church from Christ to Constantine*, 242.
19 J. Stevenson, ed., *A New Eusebius* (London: S.P.C.K), 398.
20 John Ernest Leonard Outon and Henry Chadwick, *Alexandrian Christianity* (Philadelphia: The Westminster Press, 1954), 16.
21 Ibid.,19.
22 Ibid., 21.
23 Ibid., 171.
24 Ibid., 173.
25 Persons paid to kill and perform in ancient Roman arenas
26 Ibid., 245.
27 Ibid., 245.
28 drying up
29 Isichei, *A History of Christianity in Africa*, 26.
30 Latourette, *A History of Christianity*, rev. ed., 250.
31 Browning, *A Dictionary of the Bible*, 77.
32 Kenneth Scott Latourette, *A History of Christianity* (New York: Harper & Row, 1953), 77.
33 The ancient Egyptian god of the lower world and judge of the dead
34 Isichei, *A History of Christianity in Africa*, 26f.
35 A religious life of self denial

36 Ibid., 27.
37 Freeman-Grenville, *The New Atlas of African History*, 28.
38 Ibid., 26.
39 Isichei, *A History of Christianity in Africa*, 28.
40 Ibid.
41 Ibid., 28
42 Freeman-Grenville, *The New Atlas of African History*, 26.
43 Tillich, *A History of Christian Thought*, 86.
44 Van A. Harvey, *A Handbook of Theological Terms* (New York: Macmillan, 1964), 154.
45 Freeman-Grenville, *The New Atlas of African History*, 36.
46 Freeman-Grenville, *The New Atlas of African History*, 38.
47 Freeman-Grenville, *The New Atlas of African History*, 20.
48 Elizabeth Isichei, *A History of Christianity in Africa*, 34.
49 The indigenous peoples of North Africa west of the Nile
50 Ibid.
51 William Barclay, *The Acts of the Apostles*, rev. ed. (Philadelphia: Westminster Press, 1976), 98.
52 Sindima, *Drums of Redemption*, 6.
53 Ibid., 22.
54 Isichei, *A History of Christianity in Africa*, 15.
55 Stephen Neil, *A History of Christian Missions* (New York: Penguin Books, 1964), 37.
56 Isichei, *The History of Christianity in Africa*, 34.
57 Sindima, *Drums of Redemption*, 7.
58 W. H. C. Fred, *The Early Church* (New York: J. B. Lippincott, 1966), 92.
59 Tony Lane, *The Lion Concise Book of Christian Thought* (Sydney: A Lion Book, 1984), 17f.
60 Fred, *The Early Church*, 92.
61 Tony Lane, *The Lion Concise Book of Christian Thought*, 18._
62 Sindima, *Drums of Redemption*, 7.
63 Lane, *The Lion Concise Book of Christian Thought*, 18.
64 Fred, *The Early Church*, 92.
65 Lane, *The Lion Concise Book of Christian Thought*, 25.
66 Ibid., 26.
67 Ibid., 25.
68 Ibid., 40.
69 Isichei, *A History of Christianity in Africa*, 37.
70 Neill, *A History of Christian Missions*, 37.
71 Ibid.
72 Roland H. Bainton, *Christendom*, Vol. I (New York: Harper & Row, 1966), 114.
73 *Illustrated Encyclopedia*, Vol. 6 (New York: Illustrated World Encyclopedia, 1971), 1866.
74 Ronald Oliver and J. D. Fage, *A Short History of Africa* (Penguin Books, 1990), 28.
75 Sindima, *Drums of Redemption*, 3.
76 Ibid., 34.
77 G. B. Caird, *Saint Luke* (Penguin Books, 1968), 16.
78 A term Luke uses to refer to Gentile spiritual seekers who were drawn to beliefs of the Jews but were not total converts. See Acts 13:16 and 13:26.
79 Eusebius, *The History of the Church from Christ to Constantine* (New York: Dorset Press, 1984), 74.
80 Sindima, *Drums of Salvation*, 33.
81 Freeman-Grenville, *The New Atlas of African History*, 28.

82 Noble, *The Redemption of Africa*, 27.
83 bid.
84 Elizabeth Isichei, *A History of Christianity in Africa* (Grand Rapids: William B. Eerdmans, 1995), 33.
85 Williston Walker, *A History of the Christian Church* (New York: Charles Scribner's Sons, 1959), 144.
86 Andrian Hastings, *A History of African Christianity* 1950–1975 (Cambridge: Cambridge University Press, 1979), 38.
87 Isichei, *A History of Christianity in Africa*, 33.
88 Ibid., 31.
89 Ibid., 49.
90 Ibid.
91 "Ethiopian Christianity: A History of the Christian Church in Ethiopia" (http:www.bethel/letnie/EthiopiaHomepage.html) 3ff.
92 Freeman-Grenville, *The New Atlas of African History*, 36.
93 Beetham, *Christianity and the New Africa*, 7.
94 Isichei, *A History of Christianity in Africa*, 51.
95 Sindima, *Drums of Redemption*, 40.
96 *Illustrated World Encyclopedia*, Vol. 8, (New York: Illustrated World Encyclopedia, 1971), 2551.
97 A Moor is a member of a Muslim people of mixed Arab and Berber descent living in North West Africa.
98 G. S. P. Freeman-Grenville, *The New Atlas of African History* (New York: Simon & Schuster, 1991), 66.
99 J. Kofi Agheti, *West African Church History* (Leiden: E. J. Brill, 1986), 3.
100 Ibid., 3ff.
101 T. Walter Wallbank and Alastair M. Taylor, *Civilization Past and Present*, Vol. I, 4th ed. (Chicago: Scott Foresman and Company, 1960), 558.
102 Ibid., 557.
103 Ibid., 557.
104 T. A. Beetham, *Christianity and the New Africa* (London: Pall Mall Press, 1967), 7f.
105 Roland Oliver and J. D. Fage, *A Short History of Africa* (Penguin Books, 1990), 106.
106 Ibid.
107 G. S. P. Freeman-Grenville, *The New Atlas of African History* (New York: Simon & Schuster, 1991), 66.
108 Oliver & Fage, *A Short History of Africa*, 107.
109 Ibid.
110 Chancellor Williams, *The Destruction of Black Civilization* (Chicago: Third World Press, 1987), 247.
111 *Angola: A Symposium View of a Revolt* (London: Oxford University Press, 1962), 50.
112 Ibid.
113 Ibid.
114 Ibid.
115 Isichei, *A History of Christianity in Africa*, 66.
116 Ibid., 64.
117 Ibid.
118 Ibid., 66.
119 Ibid.
120 Ibid., 65.

121 Ibid., 66.
122 Ibid., 64.
123 Ibid., 66.
124 Ibid., 66.
125 Oliver and Page, *A Short History of Africa*, 101.
126 Ibid., 103.
127 Ibid.
128 Freeman-Grenville, *The New Atlas of African History*, 82.
129 Ibid.
130 Ibid., 92.
131 Freeman-Grenville, *The New Atlas of African History*, 82.
132 Ibid.
133 *Illustrated World Encyclopedia*, Vol. 13, 4335.
134 Freeman-Grenville, *The New Atlas of African History*, 92.
135 Ibid., 92.
136 Freeman-Grenville, *The New Atlas of African History*, 92.
137 Oliver and Fage, *A Short History of Africa*, 120.
138 Ibid., 121.
139 Ibid., 121.
140 Ibid., 121.
141 Freeman-Grenville, *A New Atlas of African History*, 92.
142 Ibid., 121.
143 Freeman-Grenville, *A New Atlas of African History*, 92.
144 Oliver and Fage, *A Short History of Africa*, 122.
145 Ibid., 122f.
146 Ibid., 123.
147 Ibid., 123.
148 Ibid., 123.
149 Ibid., 123.
150 Oliver and Fage, *A Short History of Africa*, 160.
151 Ibid., 161.
152 Ibid.
153 Ibid.
154 Ibid.
155 Ibid., 161f.
156 African Diaspora refers to the dispersion or scattering of Africans and their descendants to places throughout the world, originally from slavery, later in search of education.
157 *Problems and Promises of Africa* (Nairobi: AACC, 1993), 34.
158 Ibid., 32.
159 W. R. Browning, *A Dictionary of the Bible* (Oxford: Oxford University Press, 1996), 295.
160 Ibid.
161 John Wesley Zwomunondiita Kurewa, *Preaching and Cultural Identity* (Nashville: Abingdon Press, 2000), 61.
162 Ibid.
163 Clyde L. Manschreck, *A History of Christianity* (Englewood, New Jersey: Prentice-Hall, 1964), 263.
164 Ibid., 264.
165 Ibid., 263.

166 Ibid., 263.
167 Ibid., 268.
168 Ibid., 268.
169 Ibid., 269.
170 Ibid., 269.
171 Ibid.
172 Stephen Neill, A *History of Christian Missions* (New York: Penguin Books, 1964), 251.
173 Ibid.
174 Ibid.
175 Walter Phelps Hall, Robert Greenhalgh Albion, and Jennie Barnes Pope, A *History of England and the Empire-Commonwealth*, 4th ed. (Boston: Ginn and Company, 1961), 353.
176 Williston Walker, A *History of the Christian Church*, rev. ed. (New York: Charles Scribner's Sons, 1959), 455.
177 Ibid.
178 Ibid.
179 Ibid.
180 Ibid.
181 Ibid., 269.
182 Ibid., 270.
183 Neill, A *History of Christian Missions*, 25.
184 Manschreck, A *History of Christianity*, 413ff.
185 Neill, A *History of Christian Missions*, 252.
186 Ibid., 252.
187 Umphrey Lee and William Warren Sweet, A *Short History of Methodism* (Nashville: Abingdon Press, 1954), 65.
188 Frederic Perry Noble, *The Redemption of Africa* (Chicago: Fleming H. Revell, 1899), 286.
189 MRMC (1919), 33f._
190 T. A. Beetham, *Christianity and the New Africa* (London: Pall Mall Press, 1967), 12.
191 Ibid., 270.
192 Ibid., 205.
193 Harvey J. Sindima, *Drums of Redemption* (London: Praeger, 1999), 102.
194 T. O. Ranger, *State and Church in Southern Rhodesia*, 1919–1939 (Salisbury: The Central Africa Historical Association, 1958), 7.
195 Harvey J. Sindima, *Drums of Redemption*, 75f.
196 Paul Gifford, *African Christianity* (Bloomington: Indiana University Press, 1998), 62ff.
197 John W. Z. Kurewa, "Evangelism and Church Growth in Africa," unpublished article, 2008,14ff.
198 Gifford, *African Christianity*, 184.
199 Ibid., 185.
200 Ibid.
201 Ibid., 186.
202 Ibid.
203 Ibid.
204 Alva I. Cox, *Christian Education in the Church Today* (Nashville: Graded Press, 1965), 34.
205 Rupert E. Davies, *Methodism* (Penguin Books, 1963), 65.
206 Ibid., 68.
207 Ibid., 68.
208 Ibid., 69f.

209 Ibid.
210 Ibid., 86.
211 Philip S. Watson, *The Message of the Wesleys* (New York: Macmillan, 1964), 39.
212 Philip S. Watson, *The Message of the Wesleys*, 35.
213 Ibid., 38.
214 Ibid., 40.
215 Ibid., 43.
216 *The Works of John Wesley*, Vol. VIII, 275.
217 James C. Logan, *Theology and Evangelism in the Wesleyan Heritage* (Nashville: Kingswood Books, 1994), 82.
218 Rupert E. Davies, *Methodism*, 73.
219 Ibid., 74.
220 Ibid.
221 *The Works of John Wesley*, Vol. VIII, 256.
222 Ibid.
223 Ibid.
224 Watson, *The Message of the Wesleys*, 34.
225 *Wesley's Works*, Vol. VIII, 472.
226 Ibid.
227 Umphrey Lee and William Warren Sweet, *A Short History of Methodism* (Nashville: Abingdon Press, 1956), 53.
228 Ibid., 54.
229 R. Shelddon Duecker and Alan K. Waltz, eds., *Tension in the Connection* (Nashville: 1983), 37.
230 Ibid.
231 Ibid., 60.
232 Ibid.
233 Gordon S. Wakefield, *Methodist Spirituality* (London: Epworth Press, 1999), 43.
234 Thomas A. Langford, *Practical Divinity* (Nashville: Abingdon Press, 1983), 116.
235 Thomas A. Langford, *Practical Divinity*, 116f.
236 Thomas A. Langford, *Practical Divinity*, 117.
237 Ibid.
238 Ibid.
239 Ibid.
240 Williams, *John Wesley's Theology Today*, 183.
241 *The Works of John Wesley*, Vol. XI, 384.
242 Ibid.
243 Langford, *Practical Divinity*, 117f.
244 Ibid., 117f.
245 Ibid., 118.
246 Ibid., 118.
247 Lee and Sweet, *A Short History of Methodism*, 75f.
248 Ibid., 66.
249 Ibid.
250 *The Book of Discipline of The United Methodist Church* 1990, 3.
251 Umphrey Lee and William Warren Sweet, *A Short History of Methodism* (1956), 68.
252 Barclay, *Early American Methodism*, 329f.
253 Ibid., 330.
254 Barclay, *Early American Methodism*, 330.

255 Noble, *The Redemption of Africa*, 305.
256 Ibid.
257 Ibid.
258 *The History of American Methodism*, Vol. II, 621.
259 Ibid., 610.
260 Ibid.
261 ECAMC (1901), 6.
262 Copplestone, *History of Methodist Missions*, Vol. IV (1973), 93.
263 Michael Kasongo, *History of the Methodist Church in Central Congo* (1998), 7.
264 ECAMC (1901), 10ff.
265 Philip S. Watson, *The Message of the Wesleys* (New York: Macmillan, 1964), 35.
266 Alva I. Cox, *Christian Education in the Church Today* (Nashville: Graded Press, 1965), 35.
267 Mortimer Arias and Alan Johnson, *The Great Commission* (Nashville: Abingdon Press, 1992), 20.
268 Alf Helgesson, *Church, State and People in Mozambique*, 59.
269 Ibid., 201.
270 Ibid.
271 MRMC (1919), 26.
272 Ibid., 28.
273 Ibid., 37.
274 Michael Kasongo, *History of the Methodist Church in Central Congo* (1998), 7.
275 Ibid., 10ff.
276 Ibid., 37.
277 Ibid., 25.
278 Samuel Dzobo, "A History and Theology of Evangelism: An Assessment of How Both Clergy and Laity Leadership Contributes to the Ministry," unpublished dissertation, Africa University (2006), 83.
279 Ibid., 84.
280 Davies, Ibid., 73.
281 Jean Ntahoturi, "Evangelistic Challenge to a Church in a Conflict-Ridden Region: An Assessment of the Evangelistic Mission of The United Methodist Church in Burundi (1962–2002)," unpublished dissertation (2004), 80.
282 Ibid., 1.
283 Ibid., 80ff.
284 Ibid., 85.
285 *The Works of John Wesley*, Vol. V, 296.
286 *Official Journal of the Rhodesia Annual of the Methodist Church* (1964), 87ff.
287 Arias and Johnson, *The Great Commission*, 20.
288 Joe Samalenge, "The Relevance of the Methods of Evangelism Used in The United Methodist Church in the Mutare District: A Case Study of Hilltop Circuit," unpublished paper (2009–2010 Academic Year), 31f.
289 Paul Mazumba, "A Critique of the Methods of Evangelism Used by The United Methodist Church in Harare: A Case Study of the Harare Central District," unpublished paper (April 2010), 34.